I0438741

FOOD AND DRUG SAFETY, PUBLIC HEALTH, AND THE ENVIRONMENT IN CHINA

HEARING

BEFORE THE

CONGRESSIONAL-EXECUTIVE COMMISSION ON CHINA

ONE HUNDRED THIRTEENTH CONGRESS

FIRST SESSION

MAY 22, 2013

Printed for the use of the Congressional-Executive Commission on China

Available via the World Wide Web: http://www.cecc.gov

U.S. GOVERNMENT PRINTING OFFICE

81–854 PDF   WASHINGTON : 2013

For sale by the Superintendent of Documents, U.S. Government Printing Office
Internet: bookstore.gpo.gov   Phone: toll free (866) 512–1800; DC area (202) 512–1800
Fax: (202) 512–2104   Mail: Stop IDCC, Washington, DC 20402–0001

CONTENTS

STATEMENTS

APPENDIX

PREPARED STATEMENTS

SUBMISSION FOR THE RECORD

FOOD AND DRUG SAFETY, PUBLIC HEALTH, AND THE ENVIRONMENT IN CHINA

WEDNESDAY, MAY 22, 2013

CONGRESSIONAL-EXECUTIVE
COMMISSION ON CHINA,
Washington, DC.

The hearing was convened, pursuant to notice, at 10:20 a.m., in room 562, Dirksen Senate Office Building, Senator Sherrod Brown, Chairman, presiding.

OPENING STATEMENT OF HON. SHERROD BROWN, A U.S. SENATOR FROM OHIO; CHAIRMAN, CONGRESSIONAL–EXECUTIVE COMMISSION ON CHINA

Chairman BROWN. The Congressional-Executive Commission on China will come to order.

Thank you for attending this timely hearing. I look forward to hearing the distinguished panelists, whom I will introduce in a moment, for being here to raise awareness about this important public health topic.

There are three new Members of the House of Representatives that have been appointed to the Commission: Congressman Frank Wolf, a long-time Virginia Republican; also Congressman Robert Pittenger and Congressman Mark Meadows will be joining. I hope the remaining appointments from both parties in both Houses will be made soon.

In recent months, the world has once again been reminded just how closely our health and safety is tied to the People's Republic of China. The current bird flu outbreak has claimed 36 lives and has spread to Taiwan. The discovery of 20,000 dead pigs floating in Shanghai and rat meat being passed off as lamb have renewed concerns about the safety of China's food exports.

Pollution in Beijing and other cities' industrial areas in China especially have reached what most would consider intolerable levels. This spring marks the height of the SARS crisis of a decade ago which took 774 lives and touched nearly every corner of the globe.

The risk to Americans has increased since we expanded trade relations with China without both providing for mechanisms to ensure safe imports and without assigning responsibility where it belongs in many cases, and without properly equipping our safety agencies with tools to ensure safe food.

In 2001 when China entered the World Trade Organization [WTO], the total amount of Chinese goods exported to the United States was slightly in excess of $100 billion. A decade-plus later,

(1)

that number has reached a staggering $426 billion, much of that food and pharmaceutical components.

From 2001 to 2012, China's food exports to the United States reportedly tripled. Between 2003 and 2011, the volume of pet food exports from China to the United States grew 85-fold.

Americans might be surprised today to learn just how much of their food, drugs, and pet food are made in China. Some 80 percent of our tilapia, 50 percent of our apple juice, and 30 percent of our garlic come from the People's Republic of China.

This increased reliance on China has had grave consequences. We know six years ago 149 Americans died after taking heparin, a widely used blood thinner linked to contaminants from Chinese workshops. Thousands of U.S. pets have died as a result of tainted treats from China.

Part of the problem is that some of our companies are all too willing to take advantage of China's lax safety standards, creating a playing field not level for our homegrown producers, putting our public health at risk without the responsibility that these corporations should take.

Just as important has been China's failure to provide its citizens basic rights. Chinese citizens lack the political freedom to elect officials responsive to their concerns. There is no free press to help bring these problems to public light. There are no independent courts to ensure officials and companies follow the law. And there is no free civil society to sustain long-term advocacy on consumer's or public health's behalf. The costs of the current Chinese system are clear, both to the Chinese people and to consumers who buy products made, manufactured, and/or grown in China.

Without meaningful and effective pressure from their own citizens, Chinese officials still too often choose secrecy over openness and accountability. Congress must also give close examination to our government agencies responsible for safe drugs and food and products and to the rules of international trade agreements to ensure we do not lower standards.

It is in some sense a perfect storm. It is the Chinese Government and society unwilling or unable to deal with these problems. It is U.S. regulatory agencies—understaffed and over-worked in many cases—that simply cannot reach into a country of 1.3 billion people and do what they need to do. And it's American corporations willing to profit but not willing to take full responsibility, or in some cases even partial responsibility, for what they are bringing into this country.

I look forward to the testimony of our witnesses. Cochairman Smith will be here we think in a few minutes, but obviously we will get started. I will introduce the two panelists.

Dr. Anne Schuchat is an Assistant Surgeon General of the U.S. Public Health Service, and Director of CDC's National Center for Immunization and Respiratory Diseases. She has extensive experience with China. She worked there on the SARS emergency response, where she headed a team at the World Health Organization's [WHO] China Office. She served as a visiting professor for the Beijing Centers for Disease Prevention and Control. She has made important contributions to prevention of infectious disease in children and has authored and co-authored more than 180 articles, book chapters, and reviews. Welcome, Dr. Schuchat.

Dr. Steve Solomon is Associate Director for Global Operations and Policy in the Office of Global Regulatory Operations and Policy, and Acting Deputy Associate Commissioner for Regulatory Affairs for the U.S. Food and Drug Administration [FDA]. He has worked at the FDA for more than two decades in various capacities, including in the Center for Veterinary Medicine as a veterinary medical reviewer, and within the Office of Regulatory Affairs.

Dr. Schuchat, if you would go first and keep your comments to more or less five minutes. Thanks.

STATEMENT OF ANNE SCHUCHAT, M.D., [RADM, USPHS], ASSISTANT SURGEON GENERAL, U.S. PUBLIC HEALTH SERVICE; ACTING DIRECTOR, CENTER FOR GLOBAL HEALTH, CENTERS FOR DISEASE CONTROL AND PREVENTION [CDC]

Dr. SCHUCHAT. Thank you, Senator Brown. I am really pleased to be able to update on how CDC's collaborations in China are protecting the health of Americans while protecting the health of China's own citizens.

CDC and China have been collaborating for about 30 years on public health priorities of global importance. We focused that collaboration on technical assistance and capacity building and we work with local, State, provincial, and national public health institutes.

A sign of the strength of our collaboration is that the Chinese have designated these public health institutes CDCs. The phrase ''CDC'' has no meaning in Chinese, but it is their attempt to model their program after what we do here in the United States.

Some of our signature programs in collaboration with the Chinese include the Global Disease Detection Center [GDD] and the Field Epidemiology Training Programs [FETP]. These efforts are aimed at training staff to become strong epidemiologists and on carrying out priority infectious disease and emergent threat investigations.

The GDD and FETP sites have trained many individuals, including 100 of China's top epidemiologists. They have, together, investigated over 500 outbreaks to try to rapidly assess situations and bring disease under control.

Another milestone in the collaborations between the CDC and China is the influenza work that we have done together since the late 1980s. A milestone was accomplished in October 2010 when the Chinese National Influenza Center became the fifth World Health Organization international reference center for influenza. China is the only one of those five international reference centers that occurs in a lower/middle income country and is really providing huge information and collaboration to the rest of the world.

As you mentioned, 10 years ago I was in Beijing during the SARS epidemic there and I have personally seen a huge change in the capacity and transparency of my counterparts in China. This is most evident in their response to the H7N9 influenza threat that is ongoing.

As you mentioned, since March this new strain of influenza has been identified in China. They rapidly reported the full genetic sequence of this new influenza strain and took intensive efforts to understand the problem and try to bring it under control.

There have been 131 cases reported so far. The last several weeks we haven't seen new cases, primarily we believe related to their closing down live bird markets, although some of the improvements may be due to seasonality of these viruses. We are not at all out of the woods with that particular strain, but we think the transparency and collaboration was very good for their response.

Another sign of their improved capacity is their expansion of their influenza work. They have increased from some 90 clinical sites looking for influenza-like illness to over 500. They have increased from 60-some labs that could characterize influenza to over 400 labs all around the country, and the sophistication of their work in influenza is much greater.

We think the investments that the U.S. Government has been making in China through the CDC have been catalytic. With about a $10 million budget that we provide, they are putting over $10 billion into their public health system. We strongly believe this is helping Americans.

In some ways China has become a model for other emerging economies in developing countries, as we see that over 80 percent of countries around the world have not yet met their requirements for the international health regulations that were beefed up after the SARS epidemic so that all countries would be more transparent and more able to rapidly respond to health threats and communicate them elsewhere.

We think China has made great strides in improving their public health systems and they have become increasingly collaborative with the U.S. CDC and other countries.

We are very grateful for the support that we have been getting to strengthen global disease detection around the world, including in China, to help keep Americans healthy and safe and we think that the world is continuing to be challenging. Microbes are constantly changing. We need to continue these investments to stay ahead of them.

Thank you.

Chairman BROWN. Thank you very much, Dr. Schuchat.

Dr. Solomon?

[The prepared statement of Dr. Schuchat appears in the appendix.]

STATEMENT OF STEVEN M. SOLOMON, D.V.M., M.P.H., ASSOCIATE DIRECTOR FOR GLOBAL OPERATIONS AND POLICY, OFFICE OF GLOBAL REGULATORY OPERATIONS AND POLICY, U.S. FOOD AND DRUG ADMINISTRATION

Dr. SOLOMON. Good morning, Chairman Brown. I am Dr. Steve Solomon, Associate Director for Global Operations and Policy at the Food and Drug Administration [FDA]. Thank you for the opportunity to be here today to discuss FDA's efforts to help ensure global product safety and quality, and our work related to China.

Sweeping economic and technological changes have revolutionized international trade over the last several decades, creating a truly global marketplace. Food and medical products and their ingredients and components are increasingly sourced from abroad.

The number of FDA-regulated import shipments has more than tripled compared to a decade ago to 28 million entry lines in fiscal year 2012.

Americans benefit greatly from this global sourcing of products. For example, U.S. consumers have access to a wide variety of fruits and vegetables year round, regardless of the domestic growing season, as well as access to drugs and devices.

At the same time, this rapid globalization of commerce poses challenges. Some products entering the United States are made or grown in countries that lack the necessary regulatory oversight to ensure their safety.

Greater numbers of suppliers, more complex products, and intricate, multi-national supply chains can introduce safety risks. Public health challenges associated with globalization have manifested themselves in products or ingredients from China.

As you mentioned, Chinese suppliers of heparin substituted a lower cost adulterated raw ingredient in their shipments to U.S. drug makers, causing severe allergic reactions and deaths. In another instance, melamine was added to vegetable protein in China and then used as an ingredient in pet foods made in the United States, which sickened and killed dogs and cats in the United States.

FDA recognizes that enhanced protection of the American public depends increasingly on our ability to reach beyond U.S. borders and to engage with other government regulatory counterparts as well as with industry and international organizations.

To address the challenges, FDA is utilizing a variety of engagement strategies. For example, FDA's international offices help to build strong partnerships with our foreign counterparts by providing enhanced opportunity for cooperation and capacity building. We now have a permanent FDA presence in 12 foreign posts in 9 countries, including China.

The agency electronically screens all imports using an automated risk-based system to determine if shipments meet identified criteria for physical examination, analytical testing, or other review. This system allows FDA to focus its resources on those imports that are most likely to pose a danger while at the same time facilitating entry of lower risk products.

FDA recognizes the need to engage in effective regulatory cooperation with our global partners. FDA is working strategically with a range of countries, including China, to provide information and training to strengthen the regulatory capacity of our trading partners. In addition to these activities, FDA is implementing significant new authorities provided by Congress that will help ensure the safety of imported products.

The FDA Food Safety Modernization Act enhances our ability to focus on preventing rather than reacting to food safety problems. It provides modernized tools to enhance the safety of both domestic and foreign food. For example, importers will have explicit responsibility to verify that their foreign suppliers have adequate preventive controls in place to ensure that the food they produce is safe.

Last year, Congress granted FDA other important new authorities with the passage of the Food and Drug Administration Safety and Innovation Act, which focuses on improving the safety and integrity of the drug supply chain. FDA is working hard to implement these new laws.

Let me turn to some specifics on China. As the number of products imported from China has increased, so have the challenges. FDA is taking several actions in response to these challenges. FDA currently has 13 officers posted in 3 locations in China: Beijing, Shanghai, and Guangzhou.

The mission of FDA's China Office is to strengthen, monitor, and help safeguard the safety, quality, and effectiveness of FDA-regulated products produced in China for export to the United States. FDA's China Office works to fulfill this mission through collaborating and capacity building with Chinese regulatory counterparts, academia, and non-governmental partners; reaching out to regulated Chinese firms to enhance compliance with FDA's standards; and conducting inspections of facilities that manufacture FDA-regulated goods.

To protect American consumers from potentially unsafe imported products, we utilize various regulatory controls. For example, when FDA finds a problem with a product, producer, or importer, FDA issues an import alert. There are currently 74 active FDA import alerts that include firms based in China. Under these import alerts, producers' products may be detained at the border and may be refused admission into U.S. commerce unless the importer is able to demonstrate that the products are in compliance with all FDA laws and regulations.

There are currently nine country-wide import alerts for China, including one for milk products and another for vegetable protein from China because of the presence of melamine.

While regulated industry has the primary responsibility to produce safe products, it is important that governments provide meaningful and robust regulatory oversight. FDA is working with China to help them improve their regulatory systems and to educate them on the new standards being implemented by FDA.

On both fronts, here in the United States and in China, FDA is pursuing a comprehensive strategy to enhance the safety and quality of imported products and establish an effective global product safety net.

I am happy to answer any questions you may have.

[The prepared statement of Dr. Solomon appears in the appendix.]

Chairman BROWN. Thank you, Dr. Solomon.

Dr. Schuchat, let's start with you. You used terms like ''sophistication is greatly improved,'' ''China's public health system is becoming a model for others''—understanding the limits of that—and that they ''answer health threats much better.'' Is that primarily applied to those dealing with infectious disease outbreaks, like avian flu.

Would you apply that to the issue of manufacturing, production, and growing in the pharmaceutical supply chain or the supply chain for pet food or any of those other issues, that they have greatly improved?

Dr. SCHUCHAT. Thank you for that question because I did not mean to imply the industrial changes or the supply chain issues. I am really speaking of their ability to rapidly detect, investigate, and respond to primarily infectious disease threats, but other unknown issues.

They did a very nice job recently looking at a problem with sudden unexplained deaths that had been occurring in one part of the country in Yunnan, and they were able to characterize the threat and figured out that it was related to consumption of a new species of mushroom. So that was not an infectious disease, but a toxic problem, but this is really the investigatory response capacity.

They have also put a lot of resources into improving the sophistication of their laboratory detection so they can do these sophisticated whole genome sequences. It was really impressive how they sequenced the new influenza strains and posted them immediately, which permitted the global community, the scientific community, to develop new diagnostic tests so that others could figure out whether they had the same influenza strain, and also to help get us a jump on the candidate vaccine/virus development so that if we would ever need a vaccine for this particular influenza strain we were further along.

Chairman BROWN. It is very different from a decade ago when you were there.

Dr. SCHUCHAT. Incredibly different. Incredibly different.

Chairman BROWN. The habit of authoritarian governments is, at least from my experience all over the world, denial of a problem first and then deflection of criticism, this did not happen here, do not blame us, or whatever. I mean, that is maybe human nature, too. What have you seen with transparency in China now on disease outbreaks like this?

Dr. SCHUCHAT. Yes. Sure. Yes. I think that the Chinese really suffered during SARS. There was global humiliation, there was loss of life, there were huge economic losses. I do think that they tried to learn from that in terms of aggressively investing in their public health capacity.

They have become more transparent in dealing with these outbreaks and communicating about them. One of the things we have done with the U.S. CDC collaboration is help with training on risk communication. The culture of ''don't talk about what is going on until everything is finished,'' it takes a long time to break that kind of culture. Risk communication is a technique we use in emergency response to tell people as much as we know as soon as we know it and try to sustain credibility rather than covering up.

This is important in public health and something that we are helping them get better at. There is still work to do there, but I do think that in more recent outbreaks they have been much more cooperative. They have invited WHO in, they have invited international experts in, to open the books to them and really share what is going on. So I would say that they have learned from their catastrophe, but like most countries there is more work to do.

Chairman BROWN. I remember a decade-plus ago when there was an earthquake in Taiwan. The Beijing Government did not give World Health authorities permission to go into Taiwan because of the peculiar political dynamics of our relations in Western and other countries' relationship with the PRC and Taiwan, that the Chinese did not give permission for 24 hours or something. Has that been an issue with Taiwan here on bird flu?

Dr. SCHUCHAT. I am not aware of it being an issue. I am not sure.

Chairman BROWN. The transparency with China has also been with Taiwan, that you can see?

Dr. SCHUCHAT. Yes. I probably do not know enough to answer that.

Chairman BROWN. Okay.

One other question. Talk to me about the central government's coordination with local governments on these issues, something that has more often than not been a problem.

Dr. SCHUCHAT. Yes. This is a challenging issue in many countries, frankly including our own. But I think the strength—the provinces are different. Some are quite strong, some do rely more on the central government. I think that it is probably a continuum, how well the coordination works. We work with all levels. Our primary counterpart is the national level, China CDC.

But I think that there is recognition from some of these really horrible outbreaks of how important coordination is and how lives depend on it. Here in the United States we exercise—we use local and State health departments. We work together on exercising emergency response and coordination. I think in China they have enough multi-provincial outbreaks that show the benefit of working together.

We have been supporting some expansion of their food-borne disease surveillance so that they can do what we do here, fingerprinting the strains of salmonella and recognizing the multi-jurisdictional outbreaks. Those are important health issues to identify but they also strengthen the need to work across jurisdictions. So we think that with their continuing investments in a public health capacity and even this food-borne disease surveillance expansion, they will get more practice working effectively across jurisdictions.

Chairman BROWN. Thank you, Dr. Schuchat.

Dr. Solomon, contrast the progress of 10 years in Dr. Schuchat's comments and what you know about that with the progress in 10 years on industrial supply chain, whether it is lead-based paint on toys or other contaminants, whether it is the pharmaceutical supply chain, whether it is pet food or any other kind of food. Contrast the 10 years of progress they have made on the infectious disease side with those questions, if you would.

Dr. SOLOMON. I think the analogy generally works that they have been on a trajectory to improve their regulatory systems. Clearly, the events of heparin and melamine damaged the product name for ''Made in China'' and caused significant new thinking among their regulators and some changes in their regulatory systems that we continue to see today.

I think 2007 and 2008 were kind of key years when melamine and heparin took place and when we signed agreements on both the pharmaceutical side and on the food side with the General Administration of Quality Supervision Inspection and Quarantine, the AQSIQ, who is responsible for food and feed export.

So our relationship is very different today from when melamine took place. We wanted to conduct inspections at that point in time. There were issues trying to get into China to conduct those investigations, versus now where we have people stationed in Beijing that have regular meetings, monthly meetings, at the deputy director level.

Chairman BROWN. You said Beijing, Shanghai, Guangzhou. U.S. FDA posts. What does that mean in terms of size and resources?

Dr. SOLOMON. Correct.

There are currently 13 folks stationed in China, 8 are U.S. citizens, 5 are foreign Chinese nationals.

Chairman BROWN. Among the three or at each of the three?

Dr. SOLOMON. Among all three.

Chairman BROWN. Okay. What is their training?

Dr. SOLOMON. The folks based in Beijing are mostly policy analysts that are working directly with the central government. The folks in Guangzhou are food inspectors. The folks in Shanghai are drug inspectors. You may be aware that there is additional funding in the FY 2013 budget of $10 million where we are going to be expanding the number of inspectors, so we are adding seven new food inspectors and nine new drug inspectors to that list.

Chairman BROWN. The figures that I have been told is we, the FDA, inspect 2.3 percent of imported food internationally. China's number is higher or lower than that?

Dr. SOLOMON. China's number of what we do physical inspections on is around double of what we do generally with products from around the world.

Chairman BROWN. Around the world. And that is understanding USDA's [U.S. Department of Agriculture] jurisdiction is different from FDA. That is only FDA?

Dr. SOLOMON. That is only FDA products.

Chairman BROWN. So that is—I forget. One does poultry and meat, the other does fruits and vegetables.

Dr. SOLOMON. USDA regulates poultry and beef.

Chairman BROWN. Poultry and beef. You do fruits and vegetables and other processed foods?

Dr. SOLOMON. That's correct.

Chairman BROWN. And you do dog treats and pet food?

Dr. SOLOMON. We do.

Chairman BROWN. Okay. Whether that is meat-based or not?

Dr. SOLOMON. That's correct.

Chairman BROWN. Okay.

This is an unfair question but I'm going to ask it. Rate China's regulators, U.S. regulators as interacting with Chinese products that come here, come to the United States, and U.S. importers, on a scale of 1 to 10, each of them in two categories, 10 years ago and today.

So on a scale of 1 to 10, how did U.S. regulators do in terms of regulating products? It could be toys, could be food, could be pharmaceuticals coming from China to the United States. How did U.S. regulators—give me a rating there. Give me a rating on Chinese regulators and what they did, and improvements or not they made. Give me a relative number. Then U.S. companies over, say, from 10 years ago and today. That is fairly complicated and unfair, but I ask it anyway.

Dr. SOLOMON. So let me try and approach it. I think everyone is paying more attention and I think a lot of it has to do with FDA increasing the standards. So the FDA Food Safety Modernization Act is a profound change in food safety laws that is going to increase the safety of imported products and puts new burdens on importers.

So there is a foreign supplier verification program, not yet implemented but was part of the FDA Food Safety Modernization Act, but regulations will be proposed that places the burden on the importer to ensure that back in China, or any other part of the world, that produce is grown under safe conditions and that there is preventive controls at the manufacturing facilities.

Similarly, the FDA Safety and Innovation Act is changing——

Chairman BROWN. Wait. I know, I am going to keep interrupting. I apologize. How do you ensure that importers are being faithful and truthful—truthful, I guess, more than faithful—in verifying the safety of their foreign supplier?

So how do you ensure that a U.S. company that was bringing in toys where there were issues of lead-based paints, or a pharmaceutical company that relies on Chinese small companies to give them their ingredients, how do you ensure that the U.S. importer is being truthful about the Chinese producer?

Dr. SOLOMON. So it's a variety of means that take place to try and oversee it. So the supply chain, as you have stated, is very complex. So we work on improvements with the Chinese regulators on their oversight, building capacity with them. We conduct inspections of the highest risk facilities. We monitor the importers.

We have a system that has been in place called the PREDICT System that uses sophisticated algorithms to look at the importers' information and try to verify the veracity. Has this importer traditionally only brought in one product and all of a sudden they are declaring that the product is a different product?

When the foreign supplier verification program comes into place, we will be conducting more inspections of the importers, to ensure that they have to have the demonstrated records to show that the product produced, foreign or domestic products, products from other countries, was based on the preventive controls or the produce regulations that apply both domestically and to foreign producers.

So it is a complex myriad of systems. This algorithm in PREDICT is why we target more product from certain areas than others because it is using risk-based criteria that allows us to put our resources to examine products that pose the greatest risks.

Chairman BROWN. Okay. Thank you.

If there were a similar kind of problem of deaths from heparin in this country, and I do not want to be an alarmist but just the size of everything, the size of China, you would use the term ''intricate international supply chain,'' so something bad will happen here. Some people, pets or somebody will be sickened because of something coming from China again. I mean, that is no matter how well we do it, I assume. I guess you could make that assumption.

If something comparable and as horrible as heparin happened again, something that large, what would be our government's response in terms of liability for the importer, in terms of what we do with the regulatory apparatus. What would actually be the response based on the new law you talked about and based on our apparently learning something over the last decade?

Dr. SOLOMON. So a direct result of the heparin episode was to pass, last July, the FDA Safety and Innovation Act.

Chairman BROWN. Right.

Dr. SOLOMON. That additionally puts more burdens on the U.S. companies here to make sure that they have quality management systems in place that go back to their supply chain——

Chairman BROWN. And you are seeing that now? You are seeing these companies putting better traceability, trace-back on their supply chain, even into the smallest Chinese village?

Dr. SOLOMON. They are spending more attention on it. They are on a trajectory. It has got a long ways to go, but private industry is paying more attention back to their supply chain. These laws are not in effect yet, but they have clearly seen the results from heparin and they have seen the intention of Congress and FDA to enact these controls.

So we are trying to improve the quality of information, risk-based approaches to it, and there are new enforcement tools that Congress gave us. So if we are not allowed to be able to conduct an inspection in China, now those products are not allowed into the United States.

Chairman BROWN. Okay.

If that happens, if the companies are in fact doing due diligence and something bad happens, are there liability questions? Are there liability issues for those companies? I mean, would we see those companies pay a penalty for not doing what they were supposed to do, which they should have done with heparin, having a traceability, a trace-back mechanism?

Dr. SOLOMON. So civil liability, I would leave to others. But from an FDA perspective, we have increased penalties. So for example, if there is counterfeiting of products, under the new FDA Safety and Innovation Act there are now increased penalties for counterfeiting of products.

Chairman BROWN. What are those penalties?

Dr. SOLOMON. There are new sentencing guidelines that have been put in place to allow that sentencing for criminal activities of counterfeiting are now more stringent than they were before.

Chairman BROWN. Would that be U.S. executives of those companies that——

Dr. SOLOMON. That would be the responsible party for that counterfeiting.

Chairman BROWN. So if a U.S. toy manufacturer brings in products with a high concentration of lead-based paint, it is possible executives would go to jail?

Dr. SOLOMON. Once again, we need to look at the details of specific cases, but there are criminal penalties that are in place for counterfeiting or criminal activities.

Chairman BROWN. Okay. You never did give—but I know because I kept interrupting you—me numbers. Let me ask that a different way, the question—the more obnoxious question I asked a minute ago. If Chinese regulators—I will try to do it this way.

If Chinese regulators were a 5 on a scale of 1 to 10, 10 years ago, what would they be now? If U.S. regulators were a 5 on a scale of

1 to 10, 10 years ago, what would they be now? If U.S. companies, on their corporate responsibility and traceability, track-back, were a 5 on a scale of 1 to 10, 10 years ago, what would each of them be today?

Dr. SOLOMON. It is tough to sort of categorize, as I am sure you appreciate, kind of each company. They are all on a trajectory to try and improve those pieces. FDA is improving its relationship. There are issues in relation to the central government in China and the relationships to the provincial and local governments, not unlike issues in the United States where we spend a lot of time investing in and developing an integrated national food safety system.

We spend a lot of efforts trying to work with our State, local, regulatory, and public health counterparts, exercising our response teams, putting new standards in places. They have a long ways to go in trying to build that type of integrated system, but the central government is putting new laws into place, they are investing more resources, they are better understanding our new standards and requirements. There is a lot of learning that still needs to take place.

They spend a lot of time and effort focusing on testing of products. We believe the better approach is understanding manufacturing processes and controls, the process needs to be day-in and day-out controlled, so we are working with them to try and enhance their understanding that their laboratories are fairly sophisticated and can do a lot of analytical testing. But the answer is not just laboratory testing and analytical testing of products, but also ensuring that the processes are controlled to produce safe products.

Chairman BROWN. Okay.

I recognize your challenge. I know there is enough anti-government sentiment in both chambers of this body, and sometimes it is certainly unfair, that when you think about the challenge of inspecting products in a country of 1.3 billion, let alone in a country of 300 million, the challenges there, and when we are not willing to devote very many resources relative in terms of dollars appropriations to expect so much of you.

Let me pose one question. My wife and I—our children are grown—about a year and a half ago bought a dog we named Franklin, named after my favorite President, if that tells you something about my politics. My daughter said it is finally the son we always wanted, but that is a whole other story. Would you recommend that we not buy dog food for Franklin made in China?

Dr. SOLOMON. So I think most dog food is—very little dog food is made——

Chairman BROWN. Or pet treats. Let me ask, any of Franklin's diet. Would you buy none of it in China?

Dr. SOLOMON. So the safety——

Chairman BROWN. Or do you not like dogs. Do you like dogs?

Dr. SOLOMON. I do. I am a veterinarian and I am a pet owner.

Chairman BROWN. That does not mean you like dogs because you are a veterinarian. I know some doctors who do not like people that much.

[Laughter].

Chairman BROWN. I know politicians that don't like people that much. Okay. Start again.

Dr. SOLOMON. So, pet treats are not a necessary part of a dog's diet. It's not part of a necessary, balanced diet that they need to have, so I don't feed them to my dog because they are an unnecessary part of their diet.

Chairman BROWN. And you didn't let your children have candy either?

[Laughter].

Chairman BROWN. All right. Thank you both for joining us. We will call up the next panel.

Welcome. I'd like to introduce the three panelists and then hear their statements, then we'll go to questions. My understanding is Congressman Smith is voting. His arrival is, we hope, still imminent.

Dr. Jennifer Turner is director of the China Environment Forum at the Woodrow Wilson Center and a noted expert on China's environmental energy issues. Her current projects include an initiative uncovering how energy is impacting water in China, research and exchanges on U.S.-China energy and climate cooperation, and meetings and research examining environmental impact of Chinese investment overseas. She is also editor of the Wilson Center's journal, the China Environment Series. Dr. Turner, welcome.

Dr. Yanzhong Huang is a Senior Fellow for Global Health at the Council on Foreign Relations and Associate Professor and Director of the Center for Global Health Studies at the John C. Whitehead School of Diplomacy and International Relations at Seton Hall. Dr. Huang has written extensively on global health and public health in China, and U.S. relations with China. His articles and op-eds have appeared in the New York Times and Foreign Affairs. He has a new book titled, ''Governing Health in Contemporary China.'' Welcome, Dr. Huang.

Tony Corbo is Senior Lobbyist for the Food Program at Food & Water Watch, responsible for food-related legislative and regulatory issues that come before the Senate and the House and the executive branch. Mr. Corbo has extensive organizing experience, having directed major public employee representation campaigns in several States. Thank you for doing that. My daughter did that for a living for a number of years.

Dr. Turner?

STATEMENT OF JENNIFER TURNER, DIRECTOR, CHINA ENVIRONMENT FORUM, WOODROW WILSON CENTER

Ms. TURNER. Thank you for inviting me. I am looking forward to those hard questions later on.

I am sitting in Liz Economy's place, initially, here, but she and I agree on a lot of things so I think hopefully you will get some of the same or similar stories.

The Chinese Central Government is not known for its transparency. We recall not too long ago—I think you list history—in 1994 doing my dissertation work on Chinese water policy implementation, the most benign government documents were secret. Today, happily in my work at the Wilson Center, there is a lot of access. It is very exciting. I get to gather lots of data and work with organizations in China focused on solutions to energy and environmental problems. So there has been a lot of changes over the last 10, 12 years.

Another big change in the past few years. The Chinese public is demanding more openness around pollution issues, a big change from when I was first in China. After decades of these laws and targets to clean up the environment, the Chinese public actually believes they have a right to a clean environment. With the Internet, they are starting to have tools to actually demand and put voice to these kinds of claims.

They do not just have to march out onto the street; in fact, a lot of these urbanites—and they are the ones who do tend to have the voice—are finding that they can be quite effective, at least in some more recent cases like the smog that was blanketing Beijing which has been going on for several years.

Over these past few years we have seen Chinese netizens who started to put pressure and successfully demand that Beijing start measuring small particulate pollution and also use standards that are closer to the United States. They did not really like that their standard said "fair" when the U.S. standard said "hazardous, run inside."

Another good change that really has also encouraged the public to demand information is that in 2008 the Ministry of Environmental Protection passed an open environmental information measure that said you have a right to ask for this information. It is a new tool. It does not always work—not too surprising.

But then most recently in a case that did not work that has made the headlines, and I think that is striking, the Chinese news media actually criticized the Ministry of Environmental Protection for not disclosing the soil pollution survey. The survey probably has lots of not-so-happy information about soil quality in China.

The Ministry of Environmental Protection said, "Well, no, it is a state secret," then they changed their mind and said, "Well, no, it is incomplete data, we will disclose it when we get better."

But I actually think one of the real reasons they are not quite ready to disclose it is that they do not have the laws and regulations to really deal with soil pollution. What are the standards? What is the compensation? So if you release this information, the public's demand is going to say, "Well, what do we do?" We do not have the tools yet.

So it is an example that I talk a little bit more about in my written testimony, about how you have these new open information—transparency, public right to participate, but these mechanisms and tools do not always work when other parts of the environmental governance system are incomplete.

On the good news side, Liz and I both talk about Ma Jun, an environmental activist who has used government data to create online water and air pollution databases. It has gotten the attention of not just the Chinese Government, but international and Chinese businesses, sparking a kind of greening of supply chains so instead of going to the government and saying you need to enforce this, going directly to the companies—often that are owned by the government—to actually naming and shaming so they do enforce.

Taking his transparency work even further, Ma Jun has started working with the Natural Resources Defense Council in 2009 to create a Pollution Information Transparency Index. It ranked 113 cities on how well they were disclosing information. They were not doing it very well, but what's interesting, they were able to keep going back and gathering this information, doing this index, and it is becoming more of kind of an education for the city officials and how the city officials are saying, "Oh, this is a tool that we can use," because the city officials, they, too, are blanketed with this smog and it is affecting their health. So again, kind of institutions in waiting.

Public interest lawsuits are also a work in progress. In 2007, we started seeing lawyers and non-governmental organizations [NGOs] trying to bring pollution cases in the public interest, that they were not injured themselves but because the Songhua River was polluted, or more recently cadmium tailings were dumped in a rural community in Hunan province, highly toxic. What is striking is that in a 2011 case two Chinese NGOs, independent NGOs, were actually able to bring the case to court because Hunan had provisions that granted them the standing.

Now, as of January this year there is standing for NGOs and other organizations that want to bring public interest lawsuits, but as you mentioned in your introduction the judiciary is not necessarily that independent. Local courts do not maybe want to take this giant pollution case if it is a company that is giving a lot of tax to the local government.

China has created another institution-in-waiting, these environmental law courts. There are about 90 of them. They have not been taking that many hard-hitting cases yet so there is some speculation, now that there are actually rules on the book that NGOs have standing, that maybe these environmental courts could really start turning into something more effective.

I will wrap up. There are lots of NGOs, research organizations, and the U.S. EPA [Environmental Protection Agency] working with China on some of these open information and transparency laws and regulations, trying to help to build the capacity. And I think because the Chinese Government is seeing—well, because they cannot see because of the smog—that the pollution problems are costing the economy. A lot of people in my network are seeing that there is more opening to working with China on these issues.

So I am going to halt there, and I am looking forward to your questions.

Chairman BROWN. Thank you, Doctor.

Dr. Huang, welcome.

[The prepared statement of Ms. Turner appears in the appendix.]

STATEMENT OF YANZHONG HUANG, SENIOR FELLOW FOR GLOBAL HEALTH, COUNCIL ON FOREIGN RELATIONS; ASSOCIATE PROFESSOR AND DIRECTOR, CENTER FOR GLOBAL HEALTH STUDIES, SETON HALL UNIVERSITY

Mr. HUANG. Thank you, Senator Brown, for inviting me, I am honored to be here again. Ten years ago, I testified in the same place on China's SARS crisis, so I am glad to be back.

Today I am going to talk about China's public health hazards, especially in regard to its handling of public health emergencies of international concern, such as the H7N9 outbreak. Dr. Schuchat has already spoken about how China is becoming more transparent and also more collaborative in sharing disease-related information and risk communication, so I am not going to repeat what she said.

I think it would be useful for us to ask the following question: Is China's move toward greater transparency in disease-related information sharing and risk communication irreversible?

I have a very mixed answer to that question. On one hand, the government has built up its capacity in responding to disease outbreaks. It is overall compliant with the International Health Regulations, the international law that requires governments to report public health emergencies of international concern in a timely and accurate manner.

On the other hand, I also found that the central-local gap in epidemiology and laboratory capacities, that is, their capacity to correctly and swiftly identify emerging infections, could be a major challenge—especially when the gap is coupled with an authoritarian political structure. The gap could contribute to sustained coverups, under-reporting or even misreporting at the sub-national level, as we saw in 2009 during the H1N1 pandemic.

Also, when health is increasingly viewed as a high politics issue on the government agenda, the response to public health emergencies can potentially be hijacked by domestic political considerations. This we also saw in 2009 during the H1N1 pandemic. H1N1 happened at a time when China was about to celebrate the 60th anniversary of the founding of the People's Republic of China. The government did not want to ruin the party, and the socio-political stability became such a dominant concern for the government leaders and that contributed to the lingering coverup of the fatality cases of H1N1. So if you look at the H7N9 outbreak, one of the reasons behind greater transparency was that there were not that many significant political events overlapping at the same time as the outbreak.

Also, I think it is worth pointing out that China still does not have robust civil society organizations participating in the process of disease reporting, even though the International Health Regulations, revised in 2005, legitimatized the non-governmental actors' role in disease surveillance. Indeed, the number and size of health-related NGOs in China remain very small and a vast majority of them are heavily dependent upon international donors for support. Few NGOs, if any, work on public health emergencies, and most of them are focused on one area: HIV/AIDS prevention and control.

So in that sense I am not that optimistic about improved transparency and open communication in future outbreaks. In fact, if you look at the H7N9 outbreak, what worries me is not whether China is going to be more transparent or not. What worries me is the prospect of overreaction to a disease outbreak.

As I previously mentioned, when health becomes a high politics issue and the government attaches so much importance on the disease outbreak, it could lead to a bandwagon effect at the local level in policy implementation. The local leaders will try to become ''more Catholic than the Pope,'' so to speak, which could trigger the dynamics that lead to government overreaction, potentially compromising individual privacy and human rights in China. We actually saw this happen in 2009; for example, the father of the second confirmed H1N1 case had to publicly apologize for his son being sick on government TV.

Chairman BROWN. Thank you, Dr. Huang.

Mr. Corbo?

[The prepared statement of Mr. Huang appears in the appendix.]

STATEMENT OF TONY CORBO, SENIOR LOBBYIST, THE FOOD PROGRAM, FOOD & WATER WATCH

Mr. CORBO. Senator Brown, my name is Tony Corbo and I am the senior lobbyist for the Food Program at the not-for-profit consumer advocacy organization, Food & Water Watch. We were founded in November 2005. Prior to that, we were part of Public Citizen and one of your staffers had to deal with my rants down the hall on a continual basis because we were neighbors.

We currently represent some 500,000 members and supporters on a variety of issues affecting the food and seafood we eat and the water we drink. We commend you and your leadership for holding this hearing, and thank you for inviting us to share our views.

Food & Water Watch has been interested in the issue of Chinese food safety just about from our organization's inception because it was on November 23, 2005, that USDA's Food Safety and Inspection Service [FSIS] proposed a regulation that would list the People's Republic of China as a country eligible to export poultry products to the United States.

To be able to do that, FSIS would have had to have found China to have an equivalent food safety system to that of the United States. In reviewing the audits conducted by FSIS personnel, we were perplexed why FSIS was moving forward. Some of the poultry plants they visited had serious sanitation issues, and in many of the plants there were no government inspectors present. The poultry was being inspected and passed for its safety by company-paid employees.

What also seemed problematic to us was the fact that China was ground zero for several outbreaks of highly pathogenic H5N1 avian influenza that affected hundreds of thousands of birds in China, and it also killed a number of Chinese citizens. The Chinese Government had kept secret some of the early outbreaks of this animal disease.

Most of the comments that FSIS received on the proposed rule were in opposition, including comments filed by Food & Water Watch. Ironically, the only comments that were filed in support of the proposed rule came from Chinese entrepreneurs who proclaimed the safety of their poultry.

In April 2006, FSIS finalized the rule but placed some restrictions on what could be exported to the United States. China was not authorized to slaughter its own poultry to export to the United States, instead the poultry it exported to the United States had to be cooked and raw poultry had to originate from approved sources.

At the time of the rule, the only approved sources were the United States and Canada. So North American poultry slaughter facilities could send raw product to China for cooking so that it could be exported back to the United States.

We discovered through documents we received through a Freedom of Information Act request that the Animal and Plant Health Inspection Service [APHIS] at USDA was very concerned about the lack of transparency displayed by the Chinese Government of the avian influenza outbreaks in that country, so APHIS wanted to ensure that we were not importing poultry meat from sick birds.

China never certified any of its plants to export under the April 2006 rule because they were interested in exporting their own poultry products to the United States. Congress eventually took action and prohibited FSIS from moving forward with implementing any regulation that would permit the importation of poultry products from China.

China eventually filed a WTO—World Trade Organization—complaint that was eventually sustained, but even before the final WTO ruling was published the congressional ban was lifted in 2010. China was very slow to invite FSIS back to renew the audit process. The most recent audit took place in March of this year. We still have not imported any poultry meat for human consumption.

In the meantime, the number of Chinese food exports that fall under the jurisdiction of the Food and Drug Administration has skyrocketed, to the point where 80 percent of the tilapia we are consuming in the United States is imported from China, nearly two-thirds of the apple juice we consume in the United States is imported from China, over half of the codfish we consume in the United States is imported from China, and about a third of the mushrooms we consume, yes, is also imported from China.

Unlike FSIS, the FDA does not have the same regulatory apparatus to recognize exporting countries' food safety systems before they can export. While the Congress passed, and President Obama signed into law, the Food Safety Modernization Act that contains provisions that enhance FDA's ability to regulate the safety of imported food, that law has not been fully implemented.

So our primary line of defense at FDA for food imports, for food products imported under its jurisdiction, is port of entry inspection. In good years, FDA conducts inspections of about 2 percent of imported food products.

Now, I want to get back to the chicken issue to expose some holes in our regulatory system. While poultry for human consumption is regulated by USDA, if those poultry products, as you have already pointed out, are turned into pet food they fall under FDA's jurisdiction. While China has been waiting for a green light to export their poultry to the United States for human consumption, it discovered that it could still export poultry meat to the United States if it were turned into pet food.

Over the past decade, the volume of imported pet food from China has increased 85-fold. In 2007, FDA started to receive reports from dog owners that their pets were getting sick from consuming chicken jerky treats imported from China.

The FDA has issued several warnings to pet owners, urging them not to feed their dogs Chinese jerky treats. As pets actually died and more got sick from eating these products, several Members of Congress, including you, Senator Brown, called on the FDA to conduct physical inspections of the Chinese pet food manufacturing facilities.

In March and April 2012, FDA conducted inspections of those facilities in China. When FDA inspectors asked that they be able to take samples of those products for analysis in FDA labs, the Chinese Government refused.

FDA was able to stop the importation of pet treats from one of those plants it visited because of falsification of records. That plant claimed that it had been importing industrial grade glycerin from Malaysia to make its pet treats instead of food grade glycerin. We suspect that the Chinese pet food manufacturer did that to avoid paying higher tariffs.

When FDA inspectors visited that Malaysian ingredients manufacturer in August 2012, they were able to take samples of the plant's products so that they could be tested in FDA labs. FDA was eventually able to confirm that food grade glycerin was actually being used in those pet treats.

To this day, we still do not know why these pets are dying and getting ill from imported pet treats from China. Certain products have been recalled because the New York State Department of Agricultural Markets found that some of the pet treats imported from China contained residues of antibiotics that were not approved here in the United States.

There have been numerous food safety scandals in China. The melamine situation and the infant formula is the most notorious. China, as has already been pointed out, does not have a free and independent consumer movement that can challenge the government's actions, or inaction, on food safety issues. As the volume of imports continues to increase in this country, we really do need to give our regulatory agencies the tools and the resources to ensure that these products are safe for Americans to eat.

Thank you very much.

[The prepared statement of Mr. Corbo appears in the appendix.]

Chairman BROWN. Thank you, Mr. Corbo. Thank you very much for your testimony, all three of you.

Dr. Turner, if we conclude that things are improving in the regulatory, environmental, and public health, with many exceptions but are generally going the right way, do you find that—you talked about state-owned enterprises in one sentence in your testimony— do you find that their behavior is better or worse than private companies in China than the whole? Can you make a judgment like that?

Ms. TURNER. No, I think that is very difficult.

Chairman BROWN. Where do you see the improvements in production, in manufacturing, and among companies? Where are the improvements and where are they least likely to improve, or is there least evidence of improvement?

Ms. TURNER. Well, I mean, it is a work in progress. I mean, we do have cases where either the environmental watchdogs call out a company that is polluting or the citizens themselves go to the streets. Also, cases you probably heard were actually—the people don't actually—when I was in Zhejiang province, actually the farmers went and ripped the factory apart with their own hands. So, that factory was closed.

But the challenge is that sometimes when there are protests, cities—urbanites used the open information to condemn a factory that is polluting, it is NIMBY [not in my backyard], and then these factories pack up and they move further inland, where the economies are not as rich and the likelihood of protest maybe is less, or sometimes the protest cycle starts again.

It is really hard to say. When I talk about Ma Jun and some of these other NGOs that Liz and I mentioned, they are still not huge in number but they have been trying to work to use the Internet to kind of highlight these kinds of problems within the industry and we are starting to see some other NGOs developing in the provinces to try to follow Ma Jun's example of using open information, creating networks of volunteers to put pressure on companies and working with local governments.

So I mean right now I don't—I mean, that's an excellent question about where we see the trends of who is improving. I think that you could see that on the East Coast in the developed areas because even the governments themselves are wanting to move the dirty industries out, so sometimes they're closed and sometimes they just move.

Chairman BROWN. The environmental movement, such as it is, I assume is more likely in the cities. There are more people, there is more education, there is more pollution. But you are seeing the origins of some protests and environmental movement in smaller communities?

Ms. TURNER. I mean, a few years back when the Public Security Bureau was reporting public protests, that in that number they were including mass protests in rural areas. We don't know the actual total number these days, but you do get Chinese news media reports talking about protests in rural areas and those often turn quite violent. The urban ones tend to be a little bit more peaceful, power numbers, and it's all on YouTube.

Again, they are in the cities and the government is concerned about that. I think that that is an area where that is—you know, mind the gap. That while urbanites are able—you know, again, even when the Chinese—like in the Beijing example with the smog, where now Beijing is—in the country they are starting to measure $PM_{2.5}$, their standards, and they are starting to say, "Okay, coal-fired powerplants are going to have to reduce their $PM_{2.5}$, empowering the Ministry of Environmental Protection to regulate them.

I mean, there are a lot of positive changes. But as this is happening, China's energy consumption is still growing like gangbusters and so a lot of that is coal. So even as China makes these improvements, you are not going to see an overnight improvement of quality.

So there are some questions. Liz talked about in her testimony about the central government being a little unsure where to go on this whole transparency issue, because while they do start taking some steps the actual progress on really cleaning up the environment could take a long time, again, even if you started now.

Chairman BROWN. Are Chinese companies, state-owned or otherwise, that invest in Africa or in the developing world generally, are they more environmentally responsible or are they less environmentally responsible where they invest outside the People's Republic of China than inside?

Ms. TURNER. Thanks for asking that question. We have actually been doing a series of meetings over the last couple of years, so we call it complex connections, looking at Chinese overseas investment. It really is a mixed bag. There are some, Friends of the Earth, Heritage Foundation that are looking at these Chinese investments, come and relate stories to me that some Chinese companies that are concerned about their global profile are starting to make decisions to be cleaner and greener.

But then you do have instances—let's think about agricultural investments overseas. Okay. Take two steps back. Big companies like the oil companies, the extractive industries that have a global name, they might be more concerned about working on their environmental profile.

We are starting to see though it's a new trend of provincial-level companies going out and making investments in the agricultural sector. These are much smaller, not as much transparency. Their names probably change every few weeks. So there is no one really necessarily minding the shop on how a lot of, particularly these smaller companies are doing overseas.

But I'm happy to say that there is more transparency and engagement, a lot of international—you know, the World Resources Institute, NRDC, and others, the Nature Conservancy, Conversation International, are working and talking to Chinese companies and government about this whole question of Chinese overseas investment and their footprint. So, they are talking.

Chairman BROWN. Okay. Thank you.

Dr. Huang, you were pretty vigorously nodding your head when she was talking about demonstrations, sometimes violent, in smaller communities. What were you thinking?

Mr. HUANG. I think in a way it reflects the response toward the environmental pollution problems in China. It reflects the part of this process in emerging Chinese civil society in a way that is similar to what was going on in Japan in the 1960s and early 1970s. The citizens' movement there actually forced the government to make concessions, to start to take environmental problems seriously.

I hope that China would follow Japan's path in that regard. While the situation in China today seems much worse if you look at the PM$_{2.5}$ level, I do hope there is a solution to the problem.

Chairman BROWN. You said, since you're not that optimistic, but let me ask you a sort of broader question. In the 1970s, I think, maybe early 1980s, there were some cracks in Soviet authoritarianism when a group of scientists and other citizens began to protest about Lake Baikal, one of the largest bodies of fresh water in the world, the deepest lake, where the Soviets had put a lot of paper mills, and in Siberia where there were not a lot of people living, some, people without much power, the central government. Some say that was sort of one of the first cracks in the Soviet system in terms of a democracy movement. Does the environmental movement sort of lead the way in China on human rights, on democracy?

Mr. HUANG. Jennifer probably knows more than I do about this. I do think that the environment-oriented NGOs are actually the most active part of the civil society in China. If you compare them with health NGOs, certainly they are more active, and they are also more effective in a way. But if you compare them with their Russian counterparts, the difference is indeed large.

We do see examples of public intellectuals, such as Hewei Fang and Li Chengpeng, who were very outspoken. But overall, I don't see that that many Chinese intellectuals—university professors, for example—are a part of the process.

In a way, I think that might be related to the government's efforts since 1989 to co-opt intellectuals by improving their living conditions and aiming to make them happy, which made them less willing to speak out against the government.

Chairman BROWN. Okay. Thank you, Dr. Huang.

Mr. Corbo, you talked about the implementation of the new food safety law being incomplete. What are the most important things that Congress should do? What are the most important parts that are not yet implemented and what should Congress do to make sure that they are? What do you suggest to us? You are an organizer, so you ought to know that.

Mr. CORBO. Yes. Well, we've tried. The major rules have been stuck in the Office of Management and Budget [OMB] for an inordinate amount of time. Now, two of the rules did manage to get out, the one that deals with preventive controls in processing and then the produce rules, but the comment periods have been extended.

When the law was passed, Congress set statutory deadlines that the major regulations, the produce rule, the preventive controls rule, the foreign supplier verification program needed to be implemented by July 4, 2012.

Here we are in May 2013 and those rules have not been implemented. As a matter of fact, the foreign supplier verification rule that got sent over to OMB by FDA, I believe it was November 2011, is still there. It has not come out in proposed form. I know that a number of Members of Congress have sent communications to the Office of Management and Budget to release those rules.

We just are perplexed as to why they are stuck there. I mean, FDA does need the regulatory apparatus in order to deal with this ever-increasing flow of imports. FDA cannot keep up with the volume and so those rules that were outlined have to be implemented and we have to get the comment period going.

Chairman BROWN. Other than poultry, what foods and drugs from China pose the greatest threat to Americans' health?

Mr. CORBO. Well, I've talked to various former FDA inspectors and they think that the medical devices we import and the drugs we import pose a greater risk because of the fact that we really do not have a handle on the manufacturing practices in China.

Food is our expertise and we are concerned. We are concerned about the safety of the food that is coming into this country. This pet treat thing is something that we originally were not going to get involved in. It just happened by pure accident that last year, after coming back from a meeting at USDA asking them what is the status of the poultry exports from China for human consumption, then when I got back to the office all of a sudden I saw this alert from FDA warning pet owners not to feed their pets Chinese jerky treats, chicken jerky treats, that set us on the path to find out what was going on here. How was this product getting in?

Chairman BROWN. Thank you, Mr. Corbo.

Dr. Turner, thank you. Dr. Huang, thank you. Mr. Corbo, thank you. We will have—I would like to enter Cochairman Smith's statement and Elizabeth Economy's statement also into the record. If any commission members have questions of you, we will get them to you quickly. Please answer them within a week.

Thank you again for being here. The Commission hearing is adjourned. Thank you all.

[The prepared statement of Cochairman Smith appears in the appendix.]

[The prepared statement of Elizabeth Economy appears in the appendix.]

[Whereupon, at 11:22 a.m., the hearing was concluded.]

APPENDIX

PREPARED STATEMENTS

PREPARED STATEMENT OF RADM ANNE SCHUCHAT, M.D.

MAY 22, 2013

Thank you, Senator Brown, Representative Smith and distinguished members of the Commission. It is a pleasure to appear before you representing the U.S. Centers for Disease Control and Prevention (CDC), one of the Nation's leading health protection agencies and an operating division of the Department of Health and Human Services. Throughout its history, CDC and its local, national, and international partners have worked to detect, respond to and prevent global health security threats. Today I would like to focus on how CDC's collaborations with China help to protect Americans' health and well-being, while supporting China's efforts to protect the health of its own citizens.

CDC'S GLOBAL HEALTH EFFORTS

CDC's global health mission is to protect and improve health globally through science, policy, and evidence-based public health action. CDC works in global health to protect the people of the United States; prevent disease; contribute to stable, productive societies; and save lives worldwide. CDC achieves its global health mission by leveraging its core technical strengths and partnerships. The Agency's world-class capacity to respond to disease outbreaks and other public health emergencies, our staff on the ground in approximately 55 countries, and our peer-to-peer working relationships with Ministries of Health, enables CDC to be on the scene early in events of public health concern. CDC strives not only to implement programs around the world to improve health, but also to build sustainable in-country capacity, institutions, partnerships, and systems to address global public health issues.

CDC IN CHINA

China is an important geopolitical and public health partner for the United States. CDC and the Chinese government have collaborated on public health priorities that affect China, the United States, and the global community for more than 30 years. CDC focuses its work in China on emerging and re-emerging infectious diseases, immunization, non-communicable diseases, emergency preparedness, laboratory systems development, epidemiology training, communications, and public health workforce development.

CDC's work in China is conducted through partnerships with Chinese public health institutions at the national, provincial and local level, as well as Chinese academic institutions and non-governmental organizations. In addition, the CDC works with American companies, foundations and universities as well as multilateral organizations such as the World Health Organization (WHO) to achieve our public health goals in China. CDC's collaborative projects across China have built strong bilateral relationships between China and the United States, and also help to shape China's own multilateral and bilateral engagements on global health. A sign of the strength of these collaborations is China's decision to designate their district, provincial, and national public health institutes "CDCs".

Since the early 1990s CDC has had at least one technical staff member assigned to China, and the earliest assignees worked on birth defects and immunization. In 2003, China was the epicenter for the global outbreak of Severe Acute Respiratory Syndrome, or SARS. Disruption in travel, trade, and local economies led to over 30 billion dollars in economic losses to affected countries. China and the world suffered from the initial lack of transparency and delays in confronting their epidemic. They subsequently invested heavily in improving their public health infrastructure, which helped them host the 2008 Olympics in Beijing and contributed to their effective response to the 2009 H1N1 influenza pandemic. Thus far, their efforts in the 2013 H7N9 case have demonstrated tremendous advancements.

CDC's Global AIDS Program office in China was established in 2003–2004 with funding from the U.S. President's Emergency Plan for AIDS Relief (PEPFAR). CDC works closely with the Chinese national response to HIV/AIDS, led by the National Center for AIDS/STD Prevention and Control at the Chinese Center for Disease Control and Prevention (China CDC). The Chinese government provides funding for anti-retroviral treatment for all eligible patients, while CDC provides technical assistance on guideline and policy development; innovative approaches to care, treatment and prevention; strategic information; and laboratory systems development.

The collaboration relies on a data-driven, evidence-based approach to prevent and control HIV, especially in high-risk groups.

Although CDC began influenza collaboration with China in the late 1980s, the Memorandum of Understanding on Emerging and Re-emerging Infectious Diseases between the U.S. Department of Health and Human Services (HHS) and the Chinese Ministry of Health helped formalize the relationship on infectious Diseases. In 2004 CDC established a cooperative agreement with China CDC in response to the emergence of human infections of avian influenza H5N1 virus. Since then, US CDC and China CDC cooperative agreements have improved China's influenza surveillance network and also strengthened influenza response capacity at all levels.

CDC's Global Disease Detection (GDD) program works to identify and contain infectious disease outbreaks before they spread globally. The China GDD program began in 2005 to strengthen China's national capacity to detect and respond to emerging threats, building on lessons learned from the response to the Severe Acute Respiratory Syndrome (SARS) emergency. I was in China to assist WHO with the SARS response in 2003, and have seen the extraordinary progress in their public health response and capacity since then.

CDC first established the Field Epidemiology Training Program, to train "disease detectives" to lead investigations and effective responses to public health threats. Through this effort, more than 100 of China's top epidemiologists are now able to respond to health emergencies in China. China's FETP began with a focus on tuberculosis (TB), and expanded to include laboratory capacity, foodborne disease, healthcare associated infections, hepatitis, non-communicable disease, and public health emergency response. FETP staff from China and the United States has helped conduct approximately 500 outbreak investigations since 2003.

Our partnership with China also now supports critical public health priorities in other countries, including Chinese staff participation in the CDC–WHO Stop Transmission Of Polio (STOP) missions, further enabling China to fulfill its goal of becoming a global health response partner.

The close collaboration between the United States and China CDC has yielded important results, including the designation of the Chinese National Influenza Center in October 2010 as one of five WHO Collaborating Centers for Reference and Research on Influenza—the only such Center in a low or middle-income country. In addition, together we have made positive strides in the capacity of the Chinese to respond to public health emergencies as demonstrated by the 2011 response to an outbreak of polio in China's Xinjiang province, which was caused by a poliovirus imported from Pakistan. China's immediate and effective response was described as "a true model response" by WHO.

China's large population and strong capacity to conduct sophisticated research has facilitated key studies that answer questions of global import. Research conducted in China by CDC with Chinese collaborators provided critical data that supported the decision of the U.S. Food and Drug Administration in 1996 to require all United States manufacturers of enriched cereal grain products to fortify those products with folic acid. As a result of this decision, the rates of spina bifida and other serious birth defects of the brain and spine have decreased significantly in the United States and in other countries that have implemented similar policies. Furthermore, continued collaboration with the Chinese using the original research infrastructure developed for the original study has allowed CDC to answer questions about the safety of the United States folic acid fortification program. Currently, plans are underway to initiate additional research using this collaborative platform to evaluate the potential of folic acid consumption during pregnancy to reduce childhood cancer. China is also implementing one of the largest community trials of salt reduction and hypertension management, which has the potential to have impact on heart disease and stroke prevention.

AVIAN INFLUENZA A (H7N9)

Right now in China, authorities have moved aggressively to limit the spread of avian influenza A (H7N9). This strain had never been detected in humans until March of this year. The government in China is working to monitor the illness, share information quickly and intervene aggressively. The support provided by CDC through our cooperative agreements for influenza has emphasized the integration of virologic and epidemiologic surveillance in the interest of obtaining the most complete picture possible of influenza activity. CDC's technical collaboration with China over the past decade has contributed to the ability of Chinese laboratory scientists to rapidly sequence the genome of multiple viral isolates of avian influenza A (H7N9), and post sequence data promptly for others to see. China has shown expertise and transparency during the avian influenza A (H7N9) response both in terms of epidemiologic information-sharing with global public agencies, as well as timely health communications to the public. These collaborative efforts are essential to the health security of both the American and Chinese people. The Chinese public health capacity is now greatly improved and our information about the evolving situation is much more complete than was the case with SARS 10 years ago.

For instance, the number of influenza like illness (ILI) sentinel surveillance sites in China has increased from 92 in 2005 to 554 in 2013, greatly expanding the geographic reach and representativeness of their surveillance network. The number of network labs capable of testing for influenza has grown from 63 to 409. China has also enhanced the complexity of laboratory tests done for characterization of influenza viruses. With these expansions comes a much greater contribution to the ability to monitor influenza activity globally, contribute viruses to the WHO Global Influenza Surveillance and Response System and to detect outbreaks and unusual cases of respiratory infection. The improved global network has not only strengthened China's preparedness, but also aided the global public health community with the detection of unusual respiratory disease activity and the early detection of avian influenza A (H7N9). The bottom-line with avian influenza A (H7N9) is that China continues to collaborate with the CDC and has welcomed United States collaboration.

GLOBAL HEALTH SECURITY THREATS

We believe the sustained support for our work in China directly protects Americans. Unfortunately, over 80 percent of countries around the world still lack the essential resources and sufficient health infrastructure to detect, assess, notify, and respond to public health emergencies of international concern.

CDC helps promote compliance and coordination for the United States and WHO member states, and supports WHO member states with limited resources to develop and fully implement essential detection and control capacities. CDC's global health resources support countries to fulfill these commitments by strengthening networks of laboratories, surveillance systems, and training programs in field epidemiology, laboratory science, and risk communication.

CDC strives to address global health security threats comprehensively through activities that work on multiple, complementary levels by detecting threats early; responding effectively; to containing disease outbreaks; communicating risks; and preventing avoidable catastrophes by working with other USG agencies to ensure the global food, drug, and medical device supply is safe. CDC partners with governments to improve the safety and security of their laboratories and other facilities that work with dangerous organisms to prevent the intentional or unintentional release of disease agents.

China has been an engaged partner in efforts to strengthen global health security, and CDC's partnership has led the Chinese government to make significant investments in their own capacity to detect and respond to health threats. However, most of the world has not made these commitments or reached China's level of capacity, and United States leadership is needed to protect Americans and the world.

CONCLUSION: THE VALUE OF PARTNERSHIP

China has been an important partner to align short-and long-term United States strategic, economic and health protection interests. The recent experience with avian influenza A (H7N9) has thus far shown that strategic investments in human capacity can yield important impacts on illness prevented and lives saved. In addition, continued deployment and expansion of resources on the ground will ensure U.S. leverage in Global Health Security as China rapidly expands its public health assets, with support from both domestic resources and other international partners. China has choices among its numerous international partnerships influencing the development of burgeoning public health system. The United States' continued involvement will ensure influence at critical points in China public health security development. Given the interconnectedness of global travel and trade, the rise of emerging and re-emerging disease threats, and the potential for deadly pathogens or products to be inadvertently or intentionally released, continued investment in technical assistance and broader partnership with China and the world remain strategically important for United States interests and global public health.

PREPARED STATEMENT OF STEVEN M. SOLOMON, D.V.M., M.P.H.

MAY 22, 2013

INTRODUCTION

Good Morning, Chairman Brown, Co-Chairman Smith, and Members of the Commission. I am Dr. Steven Solomon, Associate Director for Global Operations and Policy in the Office of Global Regulatory Operations and Policy at the Food and Drug Administration (FDA or the Agency), which is part of the Department of Health and Human Services (HHS). Thank you for the opportunity to be here today to discuss FDA's efforts to ensure global product safety and quality and our work related to China.

FDA is responsible for protecting the public health by helping to ensure the safety, effectiveness, and security of human and veterinary drugs, vaccines and other biological products for human use, and medical devices. The Agency also is responsible for the safety and security of our nation's food supply, cosmetics, dietary supplements, products that emit electronic radiation, and for regulating tobacco products. Imported products must meet the same standards as those produced domestically.

In my testimony today, I will discuss the challenges of an increasingly globalized marketplace, describe FDA's actions to safeguard the global supply chain, and discuss FDA's activities related to China.

CHALLENGES OF GLOBALIZATION

Sweeping economic and technological changes have revolutionized international trade over the last several decades, creating a truly global marketplace for goods and services. Accounting for 20 to 25 percent of all U.S. consumer spending, products regulated by FDA are a substantial component of this global economy. Food and medical products, and their ingredients and components—products that directly and profoundly affect the health and welfare of the U.S. public—are increasingly sourced from abroad. Today, FDA-regulated products originate from more than 200 countries and territories and pass through more than 300 U.S. ports. The number of FDA-regulated shipments has more than tripled from 8 million import entry lines per year a decade ago to 28 million entry lines in Fiscal Year (FY) 2012. In FY 2013, entry lines are anticipated to reach 34 million. By way of background, the Agency tracks import shipments using entry lines. An entry line means each portion of a shipment that is listed as a separate item on an entry document. As trade increases and U.S. consumers continue to demand global products, FDA's ability to ensure the safety and quality of these imported products will depend on its execution of a myriad of global engagement strategies.

Americans benefit greatly from global sourcing of products. For example, U.S. consumers can choose from a wide variety of fruits and vegetables year round, regardless of the domestic growing season. Ten to fifteen percent of all food consumed by U.S. households is imported. Approximately 50 percent of fresh fruits, 20 percent of fresh vegetables, and 80 percent of seafood consumed in the U.S. are imported. Health professionals can also draw on drugs and medical devices developed anywhere in the world, if they have been approved for use in the United States. Approximately 40 percent of finished drugs in the United States come from overseas, as well as more than 50 percent of all medical devices. Approximately 80 percent of the manufacturers of active pharmaceutical ingredients are located outside the United States.

This rapid globalization of commerce poses challenges. For example, some products entering the United States are made or grown in countries that lack the necessary regulatory oversight to ensure their safety. Greater numbers of suppliers, more complex products, and intricate multinational supply chains can introduce risks to product safety and quality. These factors also provide more opportunities for intentional or unintentional adulteration and exposure to contaminated products for consumers. I will discuss below the ways in which FDA is pursuing a comprehensive strategy to enhance the safety of imported products and establish effective global partnerships.

Many of the challenges associated with globalization manifest themselves in China. Historically, FDA has been faced with several public health threats related to imports from China. These include Chinese suppliers of heparin (a critical drug to prevent blood clots), who substituted a lower-cost, adulterated raw ingredient in their shipments to U.S. drug makers, causing deaths and severe allergic reactions. Other examples involved the addition of melamine to pet food made in China, which sickened and killed cats and dogs in the United States, and the presence of animal drug residues in seafood raised through aquaculture from China.

FDA's success in protecting the American public depends increasingly on its ability to reach beyond U.S. borders and engage with its government regulatory counterparts in other nations, as well as with industry and regional and international organizations, to encourage the implementation of science-based standards to ensure the quality and safety of products before they reach our country. FDA is working with its many partners to enhance responsibility and oversight for safety and quality throughout the supply chain.

SAFEGUARDING THE GLOBAL SUPPLY CHAIN

To address the challenges described above and strengthen protections for American consumers, FDA is utilizing a variety of engagement strategies, in collaboration with our many partners. Our efforts are in line with the 2012 U.S. *National Strategy for Global Supply Chain Security*, which emphasizes a layered, risk-based approach to achieving global supply chain systems that are secure, efficient, and resilient. In 2011, FDA released its report, *Pathway to Global Product Safety and Quality*, which outlines the Agency's strategy to transform itself from a predominantly domestically-focused Agency to one that is fully prepared for a complex, globalized regulatory environment. I would like to discuss just a few of the activities we are pursuing as part of this strategy.

International Offices and Foreign Posts. FDA's international offices and posts help to build strong partnerships with our foreign counterparts by providing enhanced opportunities for cooperation and capacity building. They also expand our knowledge base and provide a platform for inspection of foreign facilities. We now have a permanent FDA presence overseas in 12 foreign posts in nine countries. Our overseas employees are located in China, India, Latin America, Europe, the Middle East, and South Africa.

Risk-based Monitoring of Imported Products. While FDA does not have sufficient resources to physically inspect all imported shipments, even if we had such resources, physically inspecting all imports would be neither practical nor strategic. However, the Agency electronically screens all imports using an automated risk-based system to determine if shipments meet identified criteria for physical examination or other review. To enhance our ability to target high-risk products, FDA developed the Predictive Risk-based Evaluation for Dynamic Import Compliance Targeting application, or PREDICT. This is a sophisticated screening system that uses intelligence from many sources—such as intrinsic product risks, past inspection results, intelligence data, and even information about such threats as extreme weather that could spoil a shipment—to provide the entry reviewer with risk scores on every import line. PREDICT utilizes information sources that include FDA and U.S. Customs and Border Protection (CBP) data, as well as data collected from our foreign offices, foreign regulatory counterparts, other federal agencies, and our state counterparts. It also utilizes risk analyses we receive through agreements with academic institutions and international organizations. As we continue to increase data sharing with state, federal, and foreign government partners, as well as private partners, we will continue to incorporate more information into PREDICT. This system allows FDA to focus its resources on those imports that are most likely to pose a danger, while at the same time facilitating entry of low-risk products. FDA, the United States Department of Agriculture (USDA), and the Department of Homeland Security have also developed improved systems for monitoring for the potential of economically-motivated adulteration, which uses CBP and trade data.

Technical Cooperation and Capacity Building. FDA recognizes the need to engage in effective regulatory cooperation with our global partners. The capacities of governments to manage, assess, and regulate products within increasingly complex supply chains are a fundamental factor affecting product safety and efficacy. FDA is working strategically with a range of countries to provide information, tools, training, and exchange programs that contribute to building or strengthening regulatory capacity of our trading partners. I will describe later in my testimony some of our collaborations with Chinese government officials.

Implementing Major New Laws. In addition to these activities, FDA is implementing significant new authorities provided by Congress that will help ensure the safety of imported products.

    • **The FDA Food Safety Modernization Act (FSMA).** FSMA, the most sweeping reform of our food safety laws in more than 70 years, creates a modern food safety system. The new authorities increase FDA's ability to focus on preventing, rather than reacting to, food safety threats, share information with public health and regulatory counterparts, and make informed, risk-based decisions.

Earlier this year, FDA published for comment two proposed rules that would establish science-based standards for the prevention of foodborne illnesses—one on safe growing and handling practices for produce and another on prevention practices in facilities that process, handle, and store human food. These standards, when finalized, will apply to both domestic and foreign firms.

FSMA also provides other new tools to hold imported food to the same standards as domestic foods. For the first time, once the regulations are in place, importers will have explicit responsibility to verify that their foreign suppliers have adequate preventive controls in place to ensure that the food they produce is safe. The law also provides an incentive for importers to take additional food safety measures by directing FDA to establish a voluntary program through which imported food shipments may receive expedited review for importers that have taken certain measures to ensure the safety of the food they import. In addition, FSMA directs FDA to develop a comprehensive plan to expand the technical, scientific, and regulatory food safety capacity of foreign governments and their industries. One component of the plan is to address training of foreign governments and food producers on U.S. requirements for food safety.

• **The Food and Drug Administration Safety and Innovation Act (FDASIA).** With the passage of FDASIA last year, Congress granted FDA important new authorities, reauthorized human drug and device user fees, and authorized new user fees for generic human drugs and biosimilar biologics. These authorities and fees are intended to maintain a predictable and efficient review process for medical products, provide incentives for developing new antibacterial and antifungal drugs, combat drug shortages, and enhance the Agency's efforts to ensure that American consumers have more timely access to safe, high-quality, and affordable medicines.

Title VII of FDASIA focuses on improving the safety and integrity of drugs imported into, and sold in, the United States. The new authority increases FDA's ability to collect and analyze data to enable risk-informed decision-making, advance risk-based approaches to facility evaluation, partner with foreign regulatory authorities to leverage resources through information-sharing and recognition of foreign inspection, and drive safety and quality throughout the supply chain through the use of strengthened tools. For example, the law requires foreign and domestic companies to provide complete information on threats to the security of the drug supply chain and improves current registration and listing information, making sure FDA has accurate and up-to-date information about foreign and domestic manufacturers.

The new authorities provided by FSMA and FDASIA align with the strategies outlined in the *Pathway* report. Both FSMA and FDASIA promote collaboration with global regulatory partners, utilizing data systems to facilitate information-sharing and risk analytics and leveraging the efforts of our regulatory and public health partners. We are working hard to implement both of these important laws.

FDA ACTIVITIES RELATED TO CHINA

Nowhere is the shift toward a global marketplace more evident than in U.S. trade with China. China is the source of a large and growing volume of imported foods, drugs, and ingredients. During FY 2007–2012, the total number of shipments of FDA-regulated products from China increased from approximately 1.3 million entry lines to 4.5 million lines. Of the 4.5 million lines arriving from China in FY 2012, 67 percent were drugs and devices, and 6 percent were human food products. Three percent of our imported food, 8 percent of animal food, and 5 percent of drugs and biologics come from China.

As the number of products imported from China has increased, so have the challenges. There are currently 74 active FDA Import Alerts that include firms located in China. Forty of the Import Alerts concern food products. These alerts signal FDA investigators at the U.S. border to pay special attention to a particular product, or a range of products from a particular country, producer, shipper, or importer. Under these Import Alerts, products may be detained at the border and may be refused admission into U.S. commerce unless the importer is able to demonstrate that the products are in compliance with all laws and regulations. There are currently nine country-wide Import Alerts for China. For example, in September 2008, FDA became aware of thousands of infant illnesses in China associated with the consumption of infant formula reported to contain melamine. To keep these products out of the country and protect American consumers, the Agency issued an Import Alert for milk and milk products from China because of the presence of melamine. In addition, FDA continues to find residues of several animal drugs in shipments of aquacultured seafood products from China. As a result, FDA has imposed a country-wide Import Alert on all farm-raised catfish, basa, shrimp, dace, and eel from China.

FDA is taking several actions in response to these challenges. FDA has 13 officers posted in three locations in China: Beijing, Shanghai, and Guangzhou. This includes eight U.S. civil servants and five Chinese staff. The mission of FDA's China Office is to strengthen the safety, quality, and effectiveness of FDA-regulated products produced in China for export to the United States. FDA's China Office works to fulfill this mission through:

- Collaborating, capacity-building, and confidence-building with Chinese regulatory counterparts at the central, provincial, and municipal level;
- Reaching out to regulated Chinese firms that wish to export their products to the United States to enhance understanding of and compliance with FDA standards;
- Monitoring and reporting on conditions, trends, and events that could affect the safety and effectiveness of FDA-regulated products exported to the United States;
- Conducting inspections at facilities that manufacture FDA-regulated goods;
- Increasing the knowledge base and understanding of key stakeholders about FDA regulations and science-based approaches to strengthen product safety, quality, and effectiveness; and
- Working closely with other relevant offices within the U.S. Embassy and Consulates in China, such as the Foreign Commercial Service of the Department of Commerce, the Foreign Agricultural Service of USDA, and the Centers for Disease Control and Prevention of HHS.

Food and animal feed exported from China are regulated by the General Administration of Quality, Supervision, Inspection, and Quarantine (AQSIQ). This food-export system is separated from China's system for regulating its domestic food supply. On the domestic side, the Ministry of Agriculture has responsibility for primary food production, and the China Food and Drug Administration (CFDA) has responsibility for food processing, food in retail circulation, and restaurants. Until March 2013, these responsibilities had been held by three different ministries within the Chinese Government. FDA, through efforts led by its China Office, has established active working relationships with the food safety agencies in Beijing and will continue to work with key stakeholders in China to strengthen the safety of food exported to the United States by encouraging the implementation of science-based standards. On the human drug side, domestic drugs and certain exported drugs are regulated by the CFDA. Domestically, AQSIQ and the Ministry of Agriculture share responsibility for the regulation of animal drugs, animal feed, and feed ingredients.

I would now like to provide some examples of our collaborations with Chinese government officials.

In mid-April, FDA met with CFDA in Washington to discuss the substantive collaboration between FDA and CFDA across more than a dozen topic areas. While much of the strengthening of our relationship with CFDA has come through day-to-day collaboration between FDA's China Office and CFDA officials in Beijing, there are other significant ties in multiple areas across our agencies, such as:

- A working group on economically-motivated adulteration (the fraudulent substitution of a substance in a product to increase value or reduce production costs for the purposes of economic gain) meets on a regular basis by video, linking Washington-based experts with CFDA's key decision-makers.
- Experts from FDA's Center for Devices and Radiological Health now meet regularly with their counterparts from CFDA under the auspices of the International Medical Devices Regulatory Forum, as China has recently joined the Forum.
- FDA and CFDA collaborate closely under the auspices of the World Health Organization's Working Group for Member States on Substandard, Spurious, Falsely-Labeled, Falsified and Counterfeit Medicines. FDA and CFDA inspectors regularly observe one another's inspections.
- On May 21, 2013, FDA and CFDA co-hosted a workshop to enhance our collaboration in the fight against Internet-based, illegal distribution of adulterated drugs.

Other examples include:

- Between 2010 and 2012, FDA held a series of workshops on good clinical practices for Chinese inspectors who inspect sites that conduct trials to support the development of pharmaceuticals. Prior to the workshops, CFDA had few well-trained inspectors able to conduct inspections of clinical research sites. FDA's training in this area helped CFDA to establish its national clinical re-

search inspectorate. FDA regularly invites these CFDA inspectors to observe Agency clinical research inspections in China to continue to enhance CFDA's understanding of FDA requirements.
• At the request of CFDA, FDA's China Office and Office of Criminal Investigations worked with U.S. Internet-hosting companies to shut down 16 Chinese-language websites that illegally sold unapproved medical products through servers located in the United States.
• In 2012, CFDA provided to FDA's China Office a list of Chinese pharmaceutical firms against which CFDA had taken regulatory action because of their failure to comply with relevant standards for good manufacturing practices. From the list, FDA identified 61 firms that had shipped products to the United States and targeted these firms as priorities for inspection.
• FDA's country-wide Import Alert on five species of aquaculture fish has been in place since 2007, yet FDA continues to find positive samples of illegal drugs and additives from Chinese aquaculture products shipped to the United States. In November 2012 and May 2013, FDA and AQSIQ held workshops for members of Chinese industry to address concerns regarding aquaculture practices for fish farms. These workshops have significantly enhanced FDA's understanding of China's oversight system for aquaculture products, and have provided Chinese industry with a clearer understanding of FDA's requirements and practices.

CONCLUSION

Thank you for the opportunity to describe some of FDA's actions to address the challenges of an increasingly globalized marketplace and to discuss our work in China. FDA is pursuing a comprehensive strategy to enhance the safety of imported products and establish an effective global safety net.

Firms always have the primary responsibility to produce safe products, but it is important that governments provide meaningful and robust regulation. FDA is working with China to help them improve their regulatory system and to educate them on the new standards being implemented in our regulatory system.

I am happy to answer any questions you may have.

————

PREPARED STATEMENT OF JENNIFER L. TURNER

MAY 22, 2013

SEEING THROUGH THE SMOG? PUSHING FOR POLLUTION INFORMATION TRANSPARENCY AND ENVIRONMENTAL PUBLIC INTEREST LAW IN CHINA

INTRODUCTION

In the 36 years since opening up to the world, China's economy is still booming and it is easy to talk in superlatives about the country—fastest growing economy, largest and most populated cities, tallest dams, biggest consumer of coal, and the list goes on. China's rapid economic growth has lifted millions out of poverty and promoted wealth in the country, but at a major cost to the environment. China is now burdened with some of the dirtiest air and water in the world. There remain huge unknown threats in terms of soil quality, biodiversity losses, and long-term impacts of pollution on the public's health. The Chinese government has long acknowledged the growing litany of environmental woes and passed countless laws and regulations, but enforcement remains a key obstacle.

Since the mid-1980s, Chinese government and research institutes have actively engaged with bilateral and multilateral aid agencies as well as U.S. environmental NGOs, universities, foundations, and research institutes to address China's pollution and other environmental challenges. This international engagement has assisted Chinese policymakers in drafting and passing environmental and clean energy laws, regulations and standards, and led to joint researches between Chinese and international institutes. International organizations also have helped train and empower Chinese environmental policymakers, lawyers, judges, journalists, researchers, and NGOs to work on public participation, open information, and other environmental governance issues. For example, Vermont Law School, Natural Resources Defense Council, and the American Bar Association have all worked with the Chinese NGO Center for Legal Assistance for Pollution Victims to train Chinese judges, lawyers and local officials on public hearings for environmental impact assessments and public interest law cases. Over the last three decades, U.S. environmental NGOs have played a pivotal role in creating new kinds of cooperation and dialogues around environmental problems, forging long-lasting partnerships among Chinese and U.S. researchers, NGOs, and government agencies.

As the Chinese government has passed new laws and measures on environmental information transparency and public participation, the growing cohort of Chinese environmental journalists, lawyers, researchers and activists have gained more political space in which to operate and are placing greater bottom-up pressure on the government to improve China's weak enforcement of environmental laws and regulations. The expansion of ''green'' laws and the increasing accessibility to information on environmental issues in China has paved the path for a growing national consciousness rallying around the right to a clean environment, and Chinese citizens are increasingly willing to petition, complain, and protest the worsening environmental quality.

Below is a brief overview of some emerging trends of transparency, public participation, and public interest lawsuits around environmental issues in China. While there are many encouraging developments, ultimately these new policy tools are but one part of what needs to be larger environmental governance reforms in China.

DEMANDS FOR POLLUTION INFORMATION

In recent years, Northern China has witnessed major air pollution incidents. But the smog that blanketed Beijing and much of northern China in December 2012 and the early months of 2013 was particularly severe and worrying for government and citizens alike. During this time, pollution levels for fine particulate matter ($PM_{2.5}$) rose two, three or sometimes four times beyond the emergency level of 250 micrograms per cubic meter. Chinese citizens broadcasted their frustration with the smog through social media and some Chinese NGOs rented out personal air quality monitors to have citizens then post the registered ''hazardous'' readings online alongside official government air quality reports that listed the air pollution as ''fair'' or ''moderate.'' Through these public awareness campaigns, Chinese online citizens (netizens) successfully advocated for the central government to adopt $PM_{2.5}$ standards that match those being tweeted by the U.S. Embassy in Beijing. Greenpeace China and Beijing University School of Health issued a timely study that reported 8,600 early deaths from $PM_{2.5}$ in Beijing, Xi'an, Guangdong and Shanghai in 2012. The Chinese news media was highly critical of the government's failure to lessen the, literally, choking pollution. The public's extensive criticism online and harsh news media reporting were effective in prompting the government to make some of the following policy changes:

- China's State Council mandated rapid deployment of $PM_{2.5}$ monitoring and issued real-time data to the public. As of January 2013 a total of 496 monitoring sites have been set up in the 74 Chinese cities and the central government aims that all prefecture-level cities establish urban air quality monitoring program by 2016.[1]
- The 12th Five-Year Plan for Energy Development, which came out in January 2013 introduced a noteworthy and unprecedented pollution control policy target. Specifically, energy producers are required to cut small particulate emissions ($PM_{2.5}$) by 30 percent over the next five years. Coal-fired powerplants and oil companies will now be targeted for stricter regulation.
- To improve the city's dismal air quality, the Beijing Development and Reform Commission announced a new round of targets to cut coal use, capping coal use at 15 million tons a year by 2015, the end of the 12th Five-Year Plan period, which represents a 60-percent drop from the city's 2010 use.
- The central government announced plans to upgrade vehicle fuels quality and tighten auto emission standards.
- The smog incident catalyzed a new dialogue in China about how to evaluate local officials for actual environmental improvements, whereas in the past, they were recognized for installing pollution control equipment, even though the equipment may not be operating.

While Chinese government agencies have long issued ambitious statements addressing pollution, the difference in the latest air pollution case is that the general public, NGOs and the news media were more vigilant and willing to demand environmental information and accountability from officials, widely expressing and sharing their discontent online. A recent Shanghai Jiao Tong University survey of 3,400 Chinese citizens across 34 cities revealed that more than three-quarters of the respondents would be willing to protest against polluting industries.[2] Nearly 80 percent believed environmental protection should be a higher priority than economic development. [3]

SUCCESSES AND FAILURES IN USING OPEN INFORMATION TOOLS

An NGO's Success . . .

A growing number of Chinese NGOs are using open information measures and Internet ''naming and shaming'' as tools to pressure polluting industries and inattentive government agencies to halt pollution. Ma Jun, China's leading water pollution activist and founder of the NGO Institute for Public and Environmental Affairs (IPE), is perhaps the leader in using open information measures to motivate better environmental performance from governments and companies. In 2006, drawing on publically available information of polluters, IPE created online water and air pollution databases and publicized a list of polluters now numbered more than 125,000. A broad range of stakeholders—particularly international and Chinese companies— use these databases as a tool to monitor the environmental quality and suppliers' performance in China. International and Chinese companies who request audits to clear their names off of his well-publicized website often work with IPE's Green Choice Alliance—a group of 30 grassroots Chinese green NGOs who help oversee audits of the companies. The Alliance has motivated hundreds of factories with poor pollution records to publicly disclose their work plans to clean up their pollution.

Taking his transparency work a step further, in 2009, Ma Jun's NGO began working with a U.S. NGO, the Natural Resources Defense Council, to create a pollution information transparency index (PITI), which examines and ranks government performance in disclosing environmental information and respond to public appeals in 113 cities. The index is not intended to be solely a finger pointing exercise, but rather to help educate and motivate city officials to view information transparency as a valuable tool in promoting better environmental enforcement.

. . . and a Lawyer's Failed Attempt

Lawyers too are working to uncover poor environmental performance and test China's 2008 Open Environmental Information Measures, which gave citizens the right to request pollution information from government and industry. Soil pollution is a quieter environmental crisis facing China that only recently made headlines after Beijing lawyer Dong Zhengwei unsuccessfully applied to access data on the 2006 national soil pollution survey, conducted by the Ministries of Environment and Land Resources. Ministry of Environmental Protection (MEP) declined Dong's request citing the survey results as a ''state secret.'' At least three state-run newspapers (People's Daily, China Daily, and Xinhua) criticized China's environmental authorities for arguing that soil pollution data is a ''state secret'' and thus not fit for public consumption.

Dong subsequently pressed for an administrative review from MEP; but on May 8, 2013, the lawyer received MEP's administrative review decision that he still could not receive the information. The MEP justified the denial stating that the survey's information on soil pollution was only a general overview of the situation with more studies underway, and once the MEP completed its investigation it would release the results to the public.

China currently lacks the laws, regulations and standards that could guide MEP in requiring clean up and assigning liability, a gap that also could explain some of MEP's hesitancy in releasing what could be very unsettling information on soil quality. Thus, without legislation of action, the open information measures end up being simply an institution in waiting.

Although the ministries of environment and land and resources have not fully released the national soil survey results, researchers around China began publishing sobering articles on the scope of the problem. A Nanjing Agricultural University study hypothesized that up to 10 percent of China's rice may be contaminated with cadmium, identifying rice from Hunan, Guizhou, and Guangxi Zhuang Autonomous Region as being potentially the most heavily contaminated. China's oldest environmental NGO, Friends of Nature, released its Annual Report on Environment Development of China on April 11, 2013 which highlighted the growing challenge of soil pollution. This report cited Chinese studies that found 12.1 percent of China's farmland is polluted to some degree with heavy metals. The report also indicates that China is already suffering direct economic losses caused by pollution in agricultural lands, which leads to reduced grain production and raises public questions of food safety. Few NGOs have focused on soil quality and food safety; so shining a light on this area could help raise this issue's profile on the policy agenda. Thanks to the latest round of discussion on and off line about China's soil pollution, the country is now expecting a new oil pollution prevention and control law in three years.[4]

The Chinese Public Security Bureau no longer publishes the exact numbers on environmental pollution protests, but in a recent lecture on the social impact of pollution problems organized by the Standing Committee of the National People's Congress, Yang Chaofei, the vice-chairman of the Chinese Society for Environmental Sciences, stated that the number of environmental mass incidents has grown an average of 29 percent annually from 1996 to 2011.[5] Yang noted particularly that pollution incidents involving dangerous chemicals and heavy metal pollution have risen since 2010. Chinese news media frequently report on protests, particularly urbanites whose protests against polluting factories have led to closures and sometimes halted planned projects. For example, earlier this year when an environmental activist in Kunming learned about plans for constructing a refinery and petrochemicals base near Kunming to process oil from Myanmar, he started disseminating leaflets condemning the planned project. His efforts ultimately sparked a major protest in the city on May 17, 2013, which prompted Kunming's mayor to meet with the protestors and promise the local government would take their opinions into account in the city's ruling on the project.

While the growing number of pollution protests indicates a citizenry keen on demanding their right to a clean environment, many protests are ultimately more a symptom of China's environmental governance problem and will not, at least in the near term, solve the nation's pollutions. If, for example, the Chinese public was actively involved in environmental impact assessment hearings (as is required by law) many protests could have been avoided. Without a formal channel to learn of large infrastructure projects such as construction of incineration plants and oil refineries, the public is left with little choice but to protest when they learn about the project. Another weakness of protests is that the often "Not In My Backyard (NIMBY)" protests do not stop polluting behavior, but simply move it. There are numerous examples of dirty factories which face campaigns online and on the streets in east coast urbanities simply move the set-up to a poorer inland community where the cycle of pollution and protest may begin again. This, most notably, occurred after the 2007 PX protests in the city of Xiamen where city authorities moved a planned PX facility 30 miles inland.[6]

POTENTIAL OF PUBLIC INTEREST LAW CASES

November 13, 2005 witnessed one of the biggest environmental disasters in China's modern history. An explosion occurred at a PetroChina chemical plant in China's northwestern Jilin Province, spilling 100 tons of benzene into the Songhua River and creating a toxic slick stretching over 80 kilometers into the Amur River in Russia. On behalf of the endangered species and the polluted river, a group of Chinese lawyers filed a lawsuit against the subsidiary of PetroChina responsible for the spill, inaugurating a new era in Chinese environmental activism: seeking legal recourse for environmental harm through a public interest case. Though the court eventually dismissed the Songhua River Case, because it did not recognize animals and ecosystems having legal standing as plaintiffs, the case sparked a legal and policy discussion about how such cases could become a valuable tool to strengthen China's poor enforcement of pollution control laws and regulations. In August 2012, Article 55 of China's Civil Procedure Law was amended to create effective space for environmental public interest litigation that might have even allowed for the Songhua River case to receive standing.

The amendments to Article 55 of China's Civil Procedure Law grant the right to statutorily approved authorities and relevant organizations to initiate lawsuits against polluters on behalf of the public interest. In other words, the plaintiff does not need to show personal injury or loss from the pollution. This is the first time a Chinese national law recognizes public interest litigation. Another notable amendment, to China's Civil Procedure Law, allows non-judicial experts to challenge the opinion of judicial appraisers and aid Chinese court in fact finding, a move that opens up the court to new stakeholders. Because there are a limited number of judicial appraisers (judicial experts) in China, allowing non-judicial experts for testimony will effectively widen the pool to environmental experts and potentially increase the speed of the cases.

In 2011 two independent Chinese NGOs—Friends of Nature and Chongqing Green Volunteer Association—tested the public interest law by bringing a public interest law case against a mining company that illegally dumped 5,000 tons of chromium tailings next to a reservoir in western Yunnan. The toxic runoff severely contaminated the water and killed livestock and crops in nearby villages.[7]

Chinese courts often shun large pollution cases, yet the Yunnan court accepted the NGO plaintiffs in this case because of a provincial law that granted the NGOs' legal standing. The local environmental protection bureau also joined as a plaintiff, which greatly facilitated the compiling of evidence. Moreover, the NGOs successfully catalyzed considerable news media reporting on the case. Wang Canfa, founder of the Center for Legal Assistance for Pollution Victims, was quoted saying that this case was a good start for the public interest lawsuits in China. He considered this case as helpful in shaping the Civil Procedure Law Amendments.[8]

Robert Percival, a professor at University of Maryland Carey School of Law, explained at a November 29, 2012 meeting at the Woodrow Wilson Center that while China amended Article 55 of its Civil Procedure Law to allow for public interest suits, many questions still remain, particularly regarding precisely who can serve as a public interest plaintiff. Ultimately, the major challenge faced by those wishing to raise public interest suits is the courts' unwillingness to accept such cases, especially if the company in question serves as a major source of local tax revenue.

These new rules under Article 55 are encouraging developments that indicate a growing space for public interest law and greater involvement of NGOs in environmental advocacy. However, the Article 55 rules have yet to be tested in a large high profile case and will likely need more guidance from either the legislators or the courts to be fully applied. There are currently six to ten public interest environmental law cases that NGOs and lawyers are working on in China, which indicates an appetite to experiment with this new tool.

CONCLUSION

The smoggy air devouring Beijing is one prominent example of how 40 years of double-digit economic growth has exacted a huge environmental cost on China. The Chinese government's own data highlight the growing costs: the Chinese Academy of Environmental Planning (a research institute under the Ministry of Environmental Protection) reported in March 2013 that environmental degradation cost the country about $230 billion in 2010, or 3.5 percent of China's GDP. This is three times higher than MEP's estimate of pollution costs in 2004.[9] The growing costs of environmental degradation and the government's own inability to enforce existing laws will be one of the greatest challenges for China moving forward.

It is important for China to keep opening political space that allows grassroots groups, lawyers, and the general public to push for transparency, open information and public interest law cases, for these tools can create effective pressure for better environmental performance by the government and industry. However, in the long run there are many vital political reforms that China must make to truly strengthen environmental enforcement—such as creating a completely independent judiciary and empowering the Ministry of Environmental Protection. Alex Wang, a UC Berkeley researcher, argues that to substantially improve environmental performance by local governments China needs to establish hard targets for environmental quality outcomes against which officials at the province and sub-provincial levels are held strictly accountable.[10]

Pressing pollution problems that threaten China's economy have motivated Chinese policymakers to explore creative reforms in pollution control, clean energy laws, and regulations. Such experimentation has made environmental protection one of the most progressive policy and legal advocacy areas in China, particularly in terms of prioritizing open information, encouraging public participation, creating and setting up special courts, and granting political space for NGOs. Many international groups have conducted research and pilot projects that have helped build the capacity of Chinese regulators, NGOs, and researchers to develop these bottom-up regulatory tools. Of relevance for today's testimony, the U.S. EPA, Vermont Law School, Natural Resources Defense Council, American Bar Association, and other NGOs have been active in creating exchanges and conducting trainings in environmental information transparency, public participation, and public interest law. Such work strengthens China's environmental governance, which could help reduce pollution, better protect the health of Chinese citizens, and the products they consume. Cleaner skies over China also could lower the growing problem of air pollution from China impacting neighboring countries and the western coast of the United States.

Additionally, as the Chinese government improves environmental governance regulations and encourages stronger public and government watchdogs, Chinese companies will come under greater pressure to obey pollution control laws. Forcing Chinese companies to internalize the costs of pollution could raise the cost of products produced in China and potentially help level the playing field with international companies that have already been doing a better job in pollution prevention.

* * * * * * *

NOTES

[1] Xinhua. (2013, January 1). "74 Chinese cities release real-time $PM_{2.5}$ data." China Daily. http://www.chinadaily.com.cn/china/2013–01/01/content—16074893.htm.

[2] Brian Spegele. (2013, May 17). "Behind Chinese Protests, Growing Dismay at Pollution." The Wall Street Journal.

[3] Survey: Govt needs to focus more on environment http://www.china.org.cn/environment/2013–05/08/content—28766682.htm

[4] Caijing. (2013, May 27). "China will issue soil pollution prevention law within 3 years." http://www.cfen.com.cn/web/meyw/2013–05/27/content—978264.htm

[5] Jennifer Duggan. (2013, 16 May). "Kunming pollution protest is tip of rising Chinese environmental activism." The Guardian. http://www.guardian.co.uk/environment/chinas-choice/2013/may/16/kunming-pollution-protest-chinese-environmental-activism.

[6] Brian Spegel. (2013, May 17).

[7] Story of illegally dumped chromium in China wins environmental press award. http://www.guardian.co.uk/environment/2012/apr/11/poisoning-exposed-illegally-dumped-chromium-china.

[8] Xinhua. (2012, May 24). "Lawsuit demands 10 mln yuan for pollution victims." China.org.cn.http://www.china.org.cn/environment/2012–05/24/content—25461431.htm.

[9] Edward Wong. (2013, March 29). "Cost of Environmental Damage in China Growing Rapidly Amid Industrialization." The New York Times. http://www.nytimes.com/2013/03/30/world/asia/cost-of-environmental-degradation-in-china-is-growing.html?—r=0.

[10] Alex Wang. (February 8, 2013). "Airpocolypse Now: China's Tipping Point?" Green Leap Forward. www.greenlapforward.com/2013/02/08/airpocalypse-now-chinas-tipping-point/#more-684.

PREPARED STATEMENT OF YANZHONG HUANG

MAY 22, 2013

COPING WITH PUBLIC HEALTH HAZARDS IN POST-SARS CHINA

INTRODUCTION

In the past decade, multiple disease outbreaks have emerged in China, including the SARS epidemic in 2002 to 2003, the H5N1 ("bird flu") outbreak in 2005 to 2006, the hand, food and mouth disease (HFMD) outbreak in 2008, and the H1N1 ("swine flu") pandemic in 2009. In the spring of 2013, the emergence of a new strain of bird flu (H7N9) in China has once again raised global concern over pandemic risks. As of May 17, a total of 131 laboratory-confirmed H7N9 cases and 36 deaths had been reported in at least 10 provinces/municipalities.[1]

Additionally, in recent months, the concern over environmentally-driven public health hazards in China has grown. The off-the-chart level of $PM_{2.5}$—the most harmful types of toxic smog—in north China in January, the reports of the existence of nearly 400 "cancer villages" —areas where pollution has contributed to unusually high rates of cancer—in February, and the discovery of about 20,000 pigs floating down Huangpu River in Shanghai in March all prove how the public awareness (and the severity) of these environmental-health concerns are increasing.

IMPROVING GOVERNMENT TRANSPARENCY

In addressing the H7N9 outbreak, the Chinese government has, overall, been quite transparent. The health authorities updated information on the infection cases and fatalities on a regular and timely basis, and the National Health and Family Planning Commission (NHFPC), the successor to the Ministry of Health, also shared information about the disease with Taiwan, Hong Kong, the World Health Organization (WHO) as well as the U.S. Centers for Disease Control and Prevention (CDC). The central and local health authorities quickly unveiled plans involving medical and non-medical interventions to contain the spread of the virus. The government also acted promptly to calm speculation about the possible linkage between H7N9 and the dead pigs in Shanghai. While questions were raised on why it took three weeks for the health authorities to publicize the first cases, it appears that this had more to do with the difficulties of isolating a novel strain of the virus rather than being a deliberate cover-up.

The government openness and transparency over H7N9 prevention and control has been accompanied by increased cooperation with the international community. Within a week of the outbreak, China shipped the virus samples to WHO reference laboratories for proper identification and development of vaccines. The NHFPC also invited WHO experts to visit areas affected by the virus. The H7N9 samples sent from China enabled the U.S. CDC to develop diagnostic kits and a vaccine for the virus in case it spread to America. As noted by a senior CDC official, the information exchange with China has been "almost in real time."[2] Indeed, since SARS, the U.S. CDC has been in regular contact with its Chinese counterparts.

The improving government transparency in the H7N9 outbreak is in sharp contrast to its response in the initial stage of the 2003 SARS epidemic, which was characterized by cover up and inaction.[3] It is, of course, not the first time since the SARS crisis that the government is forthcoming about public health hazards. Drawing on lessons learned in the SARS debacle and driven by the revised International Health Regulations or IHR (2005), China has made tremendous investments in building core capacities to detect, assess, notify, and respond to public health emergencies. It has managed to construct the largest infectious disease surveillance and reporting system in the world and put in place a legal framework that aims to release disease-related information in a timely, accurate, and comprehensive manner. During the 2009 H1N1 pandemic, for example, the government swung into action from the very onset of the virus, and health authorities drummed up awareness of the dangers of the virus to make sure all intervention measures were widely broadcast and updates about the disease were regularly disseminated. The efforts to create a more open and transparent image can also be identified in areas beyond addressing public health emergencies. In January 2013, China began to release realtime, online data on $PM_{2.5}$ in 74 major cities, and in the following month, admitted to the existence of "cancer villages." This was considered a small but significant step because up until very recently, the Chinese government avoided making a connection between pollution and disease.

IS THE MOVE TOWARD TRANSPARENCY IRREVERSIBLE?

The move toward growing transparency is by no means a linear or irreversible one. As indicated in Anhui province's handling of HFMD in 2008 and Shanghai's efforts to identify the causative agent of H7N9, most localities in China still do not have the capability to correctly and swiftly identify emerging infectious diseases. Critical central-local gaps in epidemiological and laboratory capacities, when coupled with an authoritarian political structure, may contribute to sustained cover-up, underreporting, or misreporting at the sub-national level. Moreover, as health is increasingly viewed as a "high politics" issue on government agenda, government response to public health emergencies can be hijacked by domestic political deliberations. As the 20th Anniversary of the Tiananmen crackdown (June 4) and the 60th anniversary of the founding of PRC (October 1) were around the corner during the 2009 H1N1 pandemic, for example, social-political stability became the dominant concern of government leaders, which led to lingering cover-up, underreporting, and delayed reporting of cases and fatalities.[4]

But in the meantime, technological revolution and the revised IHR have generated additional incentives for openness and transparency in coping with public health hazards in China. The Internet-based disease reporting system launched in the wake of SARS, for example, has enabled hospitals and township health centers to directly report suspected disease outbreaks to central health authorities. Furthermore, the revised IHR, by legitimizing the role of non-state actors in disease reporting, have broadened the space of disease surveillance beyond the duty of the sovereign states.

THE ROLE OF CIVIL SOCIETY

To be sure, the government today continues to impose various constraints on civil society's engagement in surveillance and response capacity building. Not only does the number and size of health-related NGOs in China remain small, but vast majority of them are heavily dependent upon international donors for support. Few NGOs work on addressing public health emergencies and most of them are focused on HIV/AIDS prevention and control. As the 2008 HFMD outbreak and the 2009 H1N1 pandemic have demonstrated, in the absence of effective NGO participation in risk communication and policy implementation, upward and downward information flows could be hindered, and the state could have too much leeway to violate the privacy and human rights of its citizens when responding to public health emergencies.[5]

That said, a civil society facilitated by the spread of social media is increasingly having its voices heard and its action felt in China's policy process. To the extent that short text messages were widely used by the Chinese during the SARS epidemic to exchange disease related information, during the H7N9 outbreak Chinese people have increasingly turned to microblogs or Weibo for receiving and spreading such information. Popular posts written by leading public intellectuals such as Li Chengpeng and entrepreneurs such as Ma Yun can potentially force the Chinese government to take public health-related concerns and criticisms more seriously.

But such ''online vigilantism'' also runs the risk of taking on a life of its own by ''reaching a foregone conclusion without the benefit of a full investigation,''[6] which may not lead to effective, accurate risk communication. In the H7N9 outbreaks, for instance, the almost real-time disease alerts through social media and mainstream media outlets sent mixed signals on the nature of the virus in question. Also, the narrowing of time for response and alert could compromise government capacity to undertake effective measures for disease containment. Eager to come up with solutions to calm an anxious public, the government treatment and prevention guides advised the use of traditional medicines even though their effectiveness remained unknown and some had been found to cause serious adverse reactions.

HOW CAN THE UNITED STATES PROMOTE TRANSPARENCY AND OPENNESS IN CHINA

Despite its opaque and often exclusive policy process, global players and norms do have a role to play in China's domestic health governance.[7] Given the potential economic, social-political, even security implications of infectious disease outbreaks, it is in the interest of both the United States and China to collaborate closely in building disease surveillance and response capacities in China. As a global health leader, the United States should continue encouraging China to promote transparency and openness. In addition to cooperating with central health authorities in China, the U.S. CDC should consider shifting more resources to improve surveillance capacity at the subnational level. Also, while the United States should continue to provide financial and technical support to health-related NGOs in China, more attention and resources should be given to cultivating civil society groups that promote awareness, transparency and capacity building in addressing public health emergencies. Through deft use of social media, the United States could also play a critical role in elevating some ''latent'' public health problems (e.g., cancer villages) on the governmental agenda. In 2008, the U.S. Embassy began to monitor Beijing's air quality level using a devise atop its building. By following the Embassy's Twitter feed, Beijing residents became aware how serious the problem was. The growing awareness forced the Chinese government to become more transparent on the issue of air pollution. It began releasing figures on $PM_{2.5}$ in early 2012.

* * * * * * *

NOTES

[1] World Health Organization, Human infection with avian influenza A(H7N9) virus – update, May 17, 2013, at http://www.who.int/csr/don/2013—05—17/en/index.html

[2] Christina Larson, ''CDC Races to Create a Vaccine for China's Latest Bird Flu Strain,'' BusinessWeek, April 10, 2013, at <http://www.businessweek.com/articles/2013–04–10/cdc-races- to-create-a-vaccine-for-chinas-latest-bird-flu-strain>

[3] Yanzhong Huang, ''Implications of SARS Epidemic for China's Public Health Infrastructure and Political System,'' Testimony before the Congressional-Executive Commission on China Roundtable on SARS, May 12, 2003.

[4] Yanzhong Huang, Governing Health in Contemporary China (London and New York: Routledge, 2013), esp. chapter 4.

[5] Ibid.

[6] ''Why Is a 1995 Poisoning Case the Top Topic on Chinese Social Media?'' A ChinaFile Coversation, May 7, 2013. Available at http://www.chinafile.com/why-1995-poisoning-case-top-topic-chinese-social-media

[7] Yanzhong Huang, ''China and Global Health Governance,'' Indiana University Research Center for Chinese Politics & Business, Working Paper #26, May 2012.

———————

PREPARED STATEMENT OF TONY CORBO

MAY 22, 2013

Chairman Brown, Co-Chairman Smith and members of the Commission. My name is Tony Corbo, and I am the Sr. Lobbyist for the Food Program at Food & Water Watch, a nonprofit consumer advocacy organization. We were founded in November 2005 and our mission is to ensure that our food, water and fish are safe, accessible and sustainably produced. We currently represent some 500,000 members and supporters. Thank you for the opportunity to present testimony on this important topic.

INTRODUCTION

The United States is increasingly reliant on imported food. The U.S. Government Accountability Office (GAO) reports that from 2000 through 2011, the percentage of food consumed in the United States that was imported rose from 9 percent to over

16 percent, and food imports increased by an average of 10 percent each year for seven years.[1] According to the U.S. Department of Agriculture's (USDA) Economic Research Service, the food groups with the highest share of imports are fresh fish and shellfish (85 percent in 2009) and fruits and nuts (38 percent in 2009).[2]

China is a growing supplier of the United States' food imports. China is the largest agricultural economy in the world and one of the biggest agricultural exporters.[3] It is the world's leading producer of many foods Americans eat: apples, tomatoes, peaches, potatoes, garlic, sweet potatoes, pears, peas—the list goes on and on.[4] It is also a leading producer of many of the inputs used to make processed food, for example ascorbic acid, or vitamin C, producing about 80 percent of the world supply.[5]

But the poorly controlled expansion of China's economy has often been fueled by excess pollution, treacherous working conditions, and dangerous foods and products that pose significant risks to consumers in China and worldwide. China's food manufacturers often found to cut corners and substitute dangerous ingredients to boost sales.

Food safety problems in China have been making headlines around the world for quite a while, especially after several rounds of publicity concerning contamination of foods with a chemical, normally used to make plastic, called melamine. The chemical has been intentionally added to different food products in China, usually to try to artificially increase the nitrogen content in attempt to pass tests for protein levels.

In 2007, the U.S. Food and Drug Administration (FDA) received reports of 17,000 pet illnesses, including 4,000 dog and cat deaths, believed to be the result of melamine contamination in imported Chinese gluten used to make pet food.[6] Sixty million packages of pet food were recalled in the United States.[7] The potential health impacts were not necessarily limited to pet food, however, because some of the melamine-contaminated pet food was redirected to hog farms. Thousands of hogs that ate the contaminated food were put to death in an effort to keep melamine-contaminated meat from entering the food supply.[8] But the FDA and USDA still allowed 56,000 hogs that ate melamine-tainted pet food to be processed into pork, which was then sold at supermarkets.[9]

By 2008, the FDA had identified melamine in imported wheat gluten and rice protein from China (used in pet food), prompting rejections of 44 percent and 32 percent of these products, respectively.[10] While the FDA stopped these shipments, pet food imports from China continued to rise and reached 79 million pounds in 2010.[11]

Pet food turned out to be only the tip of the melamine iceberg. Because melamine was widely used in China to adulterate dairy products such as milk powder, processed food products including candy, hot cocoa, flavored drinks and, most tragically, infant formula contained the chemical.[12] An infant formula scandal erupted just before the 2008 Beijing Olympics and ultimately an estimated 300,000 infants and children in China were sickened by melamine; more than 12,000 were hospitalized.[13] At least six children died.[14]

Melamine-tainted milk was also exported worldwide. The New Zealand-based food company Fonterra became caught up in the melamine scandal through a joint venture with the Chinese dairy company Sanlu that was implicated in the melamine crisis.[15] The scandal played out across the globe, ending up in the food supplies of companies including Mars, Unilever, Heinz, Cadbury and Yum! Brands, Inc. (which owns Pizza Hut, KFC, Taco Bell and other fast food chains).[16]

While the melamine crisis may be the most widely covered Chinese food safety scandal, unfortunately it was not an isolated incident. International media sources routinely cover food safety problems originating in China, ranging from widespread smuggling of products like honey to avoid tariffs and food safety restrictions,[17] mislabeled products "transshipped" through another country but produced in China,[18] and importing countries discovering violations of pesticide or other food safety regulations.

A 2013 report by a food industry analyst found that among reported food violations in Chinese products, the most frequent cause was pesticides, followed by pathogen contamination. The report cited 32 pesticides found in laboratory testing of Chinese foods, mostly in produce, fruit and spices and noted that "economically motivated adulteration" is a persistent issue in food production in China.[19]

These food safety problems have not gone unnoticed by consumers in the United States or China. After more than a decade of increased food imports from China, U.S. consumers are extremely wary, with one 2011 poll revealing that participants picked China 81 percent of the time when asked to choose two countries they perceived as having the least food safety oversight.[20] Chinese consumers are not much more confident about their domestic food supply. A 2011 survey found that food safety is a major concern for almost 70 percent of Chinese consumers[21] and there are regular reports of Chinese tourists emptying store shelves in other countries in search of infant formula not produced in China.

One tool that U.S. consumers do have is labeling. Thanks to federal labeling requirements, country of origin labeling is required for beef, pork, lamb, chicken, goat meat, wild and farm-raised fish and shellfish, perishable agricultural commodities (fruits and vegetables), peanuts, pecans, ginseng, and macadamia nuts. But these labeling rules do not apply to processed forms of these foods, and the USDA's definition of processing is far too broad, which excludes many foods from the labeling requirement. The U.S. rules for labeling meat have also been challenged at the World Trade Organization (WTO), resulting in a process of revising the rules that is ongoing.

U.S. FOOD IMPORTS FROM CHINA

After joining the World Trade Organization in 2001, China's food exports to the United States tripled to 4.1 billion pounds of food in 2012.[22] In addition to Chinese firms exporting to the United States, U.S. food and agribusiness companies have capitalized on China's cheap labor costs and weak regulations, hoping to sell to a growing class of Chinese consumers and export to the United States.

Total U.S. food imports from China fell during the economic recession, but over the past four years, imports have increased by about 250 million pounds, a 7 percent increase from 2009 to 2012.[23] Fruits and vegetables (primarily frozen and processed) make up most of the U.S. imports from China, amounting to 1.6 billion pounds and 41 percent of imported food products. 1.2 billion pounds of fresh, frozen and processed fish and seafood products made up about a third of imports (30 percent).[24]

Most Chinese exports to the United States are fruits and vegetables that can be harvested and processed with lower labor costs in China than elsewhere,[25] undercutting U.S. farmers. As the world's largest apple producer, for example, China's apple juice concentrate exports supply a growing share of America's apple juice. By 2007, half the garlic Americans ate was grown in China, although that figure fell to 31 percent in 2011 as the recession and falling dollar dampened import demand.[26] Before China entered the WTO, the United States produced about 70 percent of the garlic Americans consumed.[27] Over the past decade, imports of Chinese garlic more than quadrupled, while U.S. garlic cultivation dropped by a third.[28]

The millions of pounds of imports from China represent a considerable portion of the food eaten by U.S. consumers. For example, in 2011:

- Eighty percent of the tilapia Americans ate came from the 382.2 million pounds of imports from China.
- The United States imported 367 million gallons of apple juice from China, amounting to almost half (49.6 percent) of U.S. consumption.
- The 70.7 million pounds of cod imported from China amounted to just more than half (51 percent) of U.S. consumption.
- The 217.5 million pounds of imported garlic was 31.3 percent of U.S. consumption.
- The 39.3 million pounds of frozen spinach represented 11 percent of U.S. consumption. (For more import quantities, see chart in Appendix I.)

Other Chinese exports include processed foods and food ingredients, products which most consumers purchase without considering where they came from. China is a leading supplier to the United States of ingredients like xylitol, used as a sweetener in candy, and sorbic acid, a preservative.[29] China supplies around 85 percent of U.S. imports of artificial vanilla, as well as many vitamins that are frequently added to food products, like folic acid and thiamine.[30] By 2007, 90 percent of America's vitamin C supplements came from China, and by 2010, China supplied the United States with 88 million pounds of candy.[31] The United States also imported 102 million pounds of sauces, including soy sauce; 81 million pounds of spices; 79 million pounds of dog and cat food; and 41 million pounds of pasta and baked goods from China in 2010.[32]

U.S. REGULATION OF CHINESE FOOD IMPORTS

U.S. oversight of Chinese food processors has not remotely kept pace with the growth in imports. Though the Food and Drug Administration prevented 9,000 unsafe Chinese products from entering the country between 2006 and 2010,[33] it is not because of vigilant inspection at U.S. borders and ports. The agency's low inspection rate—less than 2 percent of imported produce, processed food and seafood[34]—almost guarantees that unsafe Chinese products are making their way into American grocery stores.

Other importers of food from China have instituted more intensive testing regimes for Chinese imports. From 2004 to 2009, Japan tested between 15 and 18 percent of food products from China, and up to 38 percent of frozen vegetables.[35]

In 2007, the FDA's director of the Center for Food Safety and Applied Nutrition stated that the growing Chinese food exports have "outstretched and outgrown the regulatory system for imports in the U.S." [36] During the melamine-tainted pet food crisis, it took the FDA one month to even identify their regulatory counterparts in China.[37]

In 2007, China consented to allow FDA inspectors to be stationed in China, and the FDA opened its first office in 2008.[38] However, the few FDA inspectors in China were overwhelmed by the sheer size of the nations's food production, including an estimated 1 million food-processing companies.[39] Between 2001 and 2008, the FDA inspected 46 food firms in China—less than six a year.[40] After the spate of import scandals, the FDA increased inspections, but still only conducted 13 food inspections in China from June 2009 to June 2010.[41] In fiscal year 2012, FDA conducted 10 inspections of food facilities in China.[42] Recently, the agency instituted a sampling program for *Salmonella* for pet food, pet treats and pet nutritional supplements, but only for domestic products.[43] The new testing program does not cover imports, despite the large volume and troubled safety record of pet food and treats imported from China.

Meat and poultry imports are the responsibility of the U.S. Department of Agriculture. Until 2009, FSIS conducted in-depth annual on-site audits of countries eligible to export meat, poultry and egg products to the United States. The department recently announced that in 2009 it made a major change to this system by ending annual visits to exporting countries, and instead starting to rely on a "Self-Reporting Tool" for countries as a substitute to annual audit visits. With this change, USDA began conducting audit visits every three years instead of annually and the agency stopped the practice of publishing the audit results of individual foreign meat, poultry, egg plants that exported products to the United States. This weakening of oversight of foreign meat and poultry producers does not yet impact products from China, because the country has not yet been approved to ship these products to the United States. But China is in the process of being certified "equivalent" to U.S. meat inspection standards and therefore eligible to export products.

POULTRY

The USDA's actions with regard to China's interest in exporting poultry products to the United States offers a telling example of how the pressure to increase trade can leave food safety concerns as a lower priority. Currently, the United States does not permit poultry imports from China. U.S. agribusinesses have invested heavily in Chinese chicken production and processing—both to feed Chinese consumers and as a future export platform to U.S. consumers—and they have been working to get USDA approval for Chinese poultry exports to the United States.

In 2006, the USDA rapidly finalized China's request to begin exporting processed chicken to the United States the very same day as a visit from China's president.[44] This action apparently prompted China to resume negotiations over lifting its ban on American beef, instituted in 2003 after the discovery of mad cow disease in the state of Washington.[45]

Despite the Bush Administration's public blessing of Chinese chicken, the USDA's internal inspection reports of Chinese poultry facilities showed egregious food safety problems, including mishandling raw chicken throughout the processing areas, failing to perform *E. coli* and *Salmonella* testing, and routinely using dirty tools and equipment.[46] As these internal reports emerged, Congress refused to implement the Bush Administration proposal, effectively maintaining a ban on Chinese poultry imports.[47]

China contended the U.S. prohibition against chicken, produced in unsafe plants with insufficient inspection, was an illegal trade barrier. The World Trade Organization agreed in September 2010.[48] The same month, China announced it would impose high tariffs on American chicken products for allegedly being priced too cheaply.[49]

In January 2011, Chinese President Hu Jintao again visited the United States, cementing tens of billion of dollars in trade deals with the Obama Administration.[50] Shortly after this visit, the USDA announced new steps it had taken to honor China's request to export chicken to the United States.[51]

Currently, the USDA's Food Safety and Inspection Service is working through the steps to approve China as an exporter of poultry products to the United States, with the next step in the approval process expected to be completed in the fall. This process continues to proceed, even as the poultry sector in China is suffering mounting economic damage from a growing avian influenza outbreak.[52]

The processed poultry products being considered for approval are supposed to be made in Chinese plants from birds that have been sent from ''approved'' sources, including the United States or Canada, but not China. But without stationing USDA inspectors in Chinese processing plants, it will be virtually impossible to verify that these products are made from birds from approved sources rather than Chinese producers.

ORGANIC AND THIRD PARTY CERTIFICATION

Organic products from China have not been immune from food safety concerns. Organic beans and berries imported from China have been rejected by the FDA for high pesticide levels, despite the fact that synthetic pesticides are not allowed under the USDA organic label.[53] More recently, testing conducted by U.S. media outlets found pesticide contamination of an organic ginger product sold in the United States.[54]

According to USDA's National Organic Program, from 1995 to 2006, the value of organic food exported from China rose from $300,000 to $350 million and vegetables, field crops and tea were China's largest organic exports.[55] In 2006, there were 496 operations in China certified as meeting U.S. organic standards and by 2010 that number had risen to 649 operations.[56]

In the United States, the USDA sets organic standards and third party certifiers are responsible for inspecting farms and food processors to ensure they are meeting the standards. In 2010, the USDA visited China to conduct an audit of four of the ten certifiers operating there. The agency reported that conditions ''pose challenging oversight duties and responsibilities for certifying agents operating in China. Additionally, the size of China's land mass and higher financial margins in the organic industry could pose potential for fraud, especially by those outside of the organic certification system.''[57]

In 2010, USDA banned one of the third party certifiers operating in China because the organization used Chinese government employees to inspect state-controlled farms.[58] But the challenge of operating truly independent third party auditing or inspection operations in China is not isolated to organic certification.

The FDA Food Safety Modernization Act, which became law in January 2011, instructs the FDA to establish a reliable system of audits conducted by foreign governments or other third parties for imported foods. A 2012 GAO report outlines the significant obstacles to doing this.[59] FDA has struggled in the past to oversee inspection activities conducted on contract to the agency by state governments,[60] a task that should be much simpler than coordinating with third parties and foreign governments around the world. To build the infrastructure and IT system necessary to oversee third party certifiers in countries such as China, where third parties and even government agencies must be accredited by another government agency,[61] seems like it will be an extraordinarily challenging project for the agency.

CHINA'S FOOD SAFETY SYSTEM

Chinese officials have readily acknowledged the country's food system as ''grim.''[62] The country's decentralized and overlapping regulatory system has not been able to address China's sprawling food-processing industry. Repeated government efforts to reform food safety rules have so far failed to stem the tide of adulterated food. After a major food safety law from 2009 went into effect, a professor at the Chinese Academy of Governance stated that poor coordination between agencies, lackluster enforcement and inadequate government oversight hindered the enforcement of food safety laws.[63] It remains to be seen if an overhaul of the food safety system, announced in 2012, will manage to coordinate efforts government-wide and tighten food safety standards.[64]

The situation for Chinese consumers can be more dire than what U.S. and other export customers face. China usually exports the highest-quality food the country produces, leaving Chinese consumers vulnerable to the lower-quality products that remain.[65]

Reports on food safety problems since 2009 yield a long list of problems in both the domestic food supply and exported products. One persistent trend is ''economically motivated adulteration,'' or what has been described as a culture of adulteration in China's agricultural sector.[66] Melamine contamination in Chinese food continues to be a problem, with a crackdown on melamine in milk powder in 2010 resulting in 96 arrests and 26 public officials being fired[67] and U.S. regulators finding high levels of melamine in a dog food shipment in January 2011.[68] After increased attention to the problem of melamine, some Chinese dairy producers appear to have switched to a new protein adulterant that is even more difficult to detect—hydrolyzed leather protein made from scraps of animal skin.[69]

Even veterinary drugs banned in China—such as clenbuterol, administered to animals to give them leaner meat and pinker skin—remain widely used in China despite years of documented consumer illnesses from residues in meat and organs,[70] and controversies over athletes avoiding meat for fear of testing positive for the performance enhancing drug.

Honey from China has continued to be a source of controversy. Illegal antibiotics are commonly found in Chinese honey imports. China dominates the international honey market and became the largest U.S. honey source after joining the WTO, supplying more than 70 million pounds by 2006.[71] For years, regulators had closely scrutinized Chinese honey for drug residues, including one that can be fatal.[72] In 2010, the FDA seized large amounts of Chinese honey after finding illegal antibiotics.[73]

Another trend is pesticide residues that remain on fruit, vegetables and processed foods when they enter the food supply. China is the world's largest pesticide producer and exporter.[74] In 2010, Chinese authorities found a banned, highly toxic pesticide in cowpeas, a legume similar to black-eyed peas.[75] China has largely failed to address illegal or dangerous chemical residues on food, evident in its weak maximum residue levels. The United States has established maximum residue levels (MRLs) for 77 pesticides used in garlic production and 112 pesticides used in apples orchards; of these, China has only 2 and 23 MRLs, respectively.[76]

Since 2009, the Chinese government has made a point of making public displays of enforcing food safety rules, inspecting food facilities and punishing people connected with tainted food. News reports frequently reference millions of inspections of facilities and frequent "crackdowns" on particular products. A search of news reports reveals a variety of enforcement efforts:

- The scandal over melamine-contaminated infant formula led to the execution of two people and prison terms for dairy company executives.[77]
- In 2011, industry and commerce authorities reported 62,000 cases of substandard food, leading to 43,000 unlicensed operations being shut down and 251 cases being sent to the judicial system.[78]
- A 2011 crackdown on food safety violations resulted in 2,000 arrests and 4,900 businesses being closed.[79]
- The Chinese news agency Xinhua reported in June 2012 that authorities shut down 5,700 unlicensed food businesses and discovered 15,000 cases of "substandard food" so far that year.[80]
- In early May 2013, news reports described a Chinese government campaign to break up a fake meat operation, leading to arrests of more than 900 people accused of passing off more than $1 million of rat meat as mutton.[81]

Ironically, the recent discovery of more than 7,000 dead pigs in the Huangpu River was actually described in some media reports as "an encouraging step forward in Chinese public health," because it indicated that rather than sell diseased animals into the food supply, producers dumped them into the river instead.[82]

But despite the concerted effort to show that the government is tough on food safety violators, problems persist. A small sample of recent food safety problems:

- In 2010, a scandal erupted over the use of food coloring and bleach to plump up shriveled old peas so they would appear fresh.[83]
- Authorities detected plasticizers, chemicals linked to immune and reproductive system damage, in samples of a leading brand of a common distilled white liquor.[84]
- Testing by Greenpeace of 18 varieties of tea found that every sample contained at least three different kinds of pesticides. 12 of the samples showed traces of banned pesticides.[85]
- In September 2012, FDA refused 10 shipments of canned mushrooms from China due to pesticide contamination, resulting in the Chinese government halting exports of canned mushrooms to the United States.[86]
- China Central Television reported in 2012 that testing of preserved fruit from 16 different companies found excessive pigments, bleaching agents and preservatives, as well as incorrect expiration dates.[87]
- The Xinhua News Agency reported in 2012 that wholesale vegetable dealers in Shandong province were found spraying cabbages with formaldehyde, presumably to preserve them during transport without refrigeration.[88]
- A 2012 report noted that fish vendors in Beijing were using a chemical used for temporary dental fillings to tranquilize fish during transport.[89]

Another recurring theme is lack of transparency. China's food safety enforcement system lacks the transparency necessary to warn the public about dangerous products or deter dangerous food-processing practices. The USDA reports that the Chinese government zealously guards the food safety data it collects, making it difficult to impartially evaluate China's food safety performance.[90] In 2010, some officials criticized regional authorities that publicized a widespread case of pesticide adulteration rather than obeying the "unspoken rule" of keeping food safety problems hidden from the public.[91] The father of one child sickened by melamine-tainted milk powder was jailed, and eventually paroled, for his activism on the issue.[92]

Lack of transparency is also evident in an ongoing problem with imported pet treats from China. Since 2007, thousands of American dogs have fallen ill or died after eating chicken jerky treats made in China. The FDA reports "from 2003, when China first approached the USDA about poultry exports, to 2011, the volume of pet food exports (regulated by the FDA) to the United States from China has grown 85-fold."[93] In August 2012, four months after visiting Chinese processing plants that export pet treats to the United States, the FDA published inspection reports that revealed that the factories refused to allow U.S. inspectors to collect samples for independent analysis.[94] Ultimately, testing done by the New York Department of Agriculture and Markets found contamination of some of the treats with residues of an undisclosed antibiotic, triggering voluntary recalls of the products by the manufacturer.[95]

IMPORTED PHARMACEUTICALS FROM CHINA

While Food & Water Watch does not work on the safety of pharmaceuticals, we have been following some of the problems that have surfaced with the safety of imported drugs, particularly from China. In 2011 testimony before the Senate Health, Education, Labor and Pensions Committee, the Government Accountability Office noted that the number of imported pharmaceuticals has more than doubled since 2002, with China and India leading that growth. FDA was only able to conduct inspections of a very small number of foreign drug facilities that export to the U.S.[96] In 2007 and 2008, the FDA discovered that there was a large spike in the number of deaths of consumers who took the blood thinner heparin. Heparin is made from the intestines of pigs and because of the abundant supply of swine in China, it is the primary source for crude heparin for U.S. drug manufacturers.[97] As a result of investigations conducted by the FDA and the Centers for Disease Control, it was discovered that some of the Chinese crude heparin was actually oversulfated chondroitin sulfate (OSCS). OSCS can easily be confused for heparin in routine product testing. OSCS does not confer the same medicinal benefits as heparin to patients who have to take the drug and it is a cheaper substance. The FDA estimates that as many as 149 U.S. consumers died from the intentional economic adulteration of this drug.[98] The Chinese government has never accepted responsibility for the contaminated heparin reaching our shores.

U.S. POLICIES TO ADDRESS UNSAFE FOOD IMPORTS

The WTO's Agreement on Agriculture has been a failure for farmers in the United States and has encouraged the growth of export platforms in places like China that benefit from low wages and weak regulatory standards, putting consumers around the world at risk. Congress and the Obama administration must revisit the current trade agenda to make public health, environmental standards and consumer safety the highest priorities when making decisions about trade policy. Specifically:

- The USDA should restart the process of determining if China's poultry inspection system is equivalent to the U.S. system and conduct an entirely new investigation before allowing Chinese poultry products to be exported to the United States.
- The USDA needs the resources to increase current levels of inspection of imported meat and poultry. If Chinese poultry products are approved for export to the United States, the USDA should permanently assign inspection personnel to China so that the exporting plants receive regular visits by USDA inspectors.
- The FDA needs the resources to effectively inspect the growing volume of food imports from China and other countries. Congress and the Obama Administration must provide adequate funding to the FDA to increase import inspections, and to increase the rigor of those inspections to include testing for pathogens and chemical, pesticide and drug residues, and to increase inspection of processed food ingredients.
- The FDA needs the resources to conduct inspections in food facilities in China, rather than relying on third-party certifications of the safety practices used by exporting firms. The use of third-party certifications in China has already been shown to be questionable in the certification used for organic products and in pilot projects on aquaculture conducted by the FDA. This type of

system should not be used as a substitute for safety inspection by U.S. government inspectors.

• The USDA should close the loopholes in the current country of origin labeling rules and expand them to processed meats, fruits and vegetables. Congress should also require mandatory country of origin labeling for foods not currently covered by existing law, to require basic manufacturing information about where, and by what company, processed foods were produced.

I would happy to answer any questions that you might have. Thank you, again, for inviting Food & Water Watch to contribute to this discussion.

APPENDIX 1

Food Product	U.S. Imports from China (Millions of Pounds)				Share of U.S. Consumption				
	2009	2010	2011	2012	2008	2009	2010	2011	4-Year Average
Tilapia	288.3	349.5	318.5	382.2	73.2%	77.8%	78.7%	80.2%	77.5%
Apple Juice (Mil. Gall.)	451.4	463.7	342.0	367.0	69.0%	70.0%	72.3%	49.6%	65.2%
Cod	63.2	71.4	78.9	70.7	59.4%	50.0%	50.4%	51.0%	52.7%
Mushrooms, Processing	78.1	78.6	68.2	68,4	53.7%	42.7%	22.4%	17.8%	34.1%
Garlic, All Uses	245.4	234.3	226.9	217.5	23.1%	22.8%	32.4%	31.3%	27.4%
Clams	17.0	19.8	24.1	27.4	9.0%	12.7%	19.0%	23.5%	16.1%
Spinach, Frozen	32.2	32.5	36.2	39.3	16.0%	21.5%	15.3%	11.0%	16.0%
Crab	18.9	23.7	22.9	22.9	15.0%	10.4%	13.5%	14.3%	13.3%
Salmon	71.4	88.1	86.4	72.7	10.8%	11.1%	14.4%	14.3%	12.7%
Peaches, Canned	91.8	109.8	92.0	98.5	11.8%	9.1%	9.0%	8.1%	9.5%
Cauliflower, Processing	11.1	8.9	1.3	8.1	12.0%	14.6%	7.8%	0.9%	8.8%
Shrimp	97.1	106.0	94.7	78.6	8.6%	7.8%	8.7%	7.3%	8.1%
Pineapples, Canned	65.2	52.7	40.6	26.2	9.7%	8.7%	7.1%	5.8%	7.8%
Pears, Canned	53.0	57.2	49.4	50.7	7.3%	7.0%	7.6%	8.1%	7.5%
Asparagus, Frozen	1.4	1.1	0.8	0.2	10.7%	12.2%	3.4%	1.9%	7.1%
Catfish/Pangasius	22.8	17.9	10.8	7.9	2.7%	1.6%	14.4%	5.6%	6.1%
Broccoli, Processed	29.4	25.7	30,4	25.9	3.7%	4.9%	3.4%	3.7%	3.9%
Green Peas, Frozen	16.6	20.4	10.3	5.7	4.2%	3.5%	4.2%	2.3%	3.5%
Cherries, Sweet, Canned	0.1	0.6	0.0	0.3	0.0%	1.9%	8.4%		3.4%
Onions, Dried	5.5	4.3	2.8	3.1	5.9%	5.1%	0.9%	0.6%	3.1%
Apples, Canned	32.4	18.7	17.4	31.9	2.5%	3.0%	1.8%	1.8%	2.3%
Canned Tuna	18.6	17.6	40.7	52.5	0.0%	1.9%	2.1%	5.1%	2.3%
Pears, Fresh	24.3	11.6	13.8	12.4	2.8%	2.5%	1.2%	1.5%	2.0%
Strawberries, Frozen	7.1	10.8	9.1	5.7	1.2%	1.3%	0.0%	0.0%	0.6%
Mushroom, Fresh	10.6	10.6	11.4	13.0	1.3%	1.4%	1.4%	1.4%	1.4%
Artichoke, All Uses	3.5	2.1	2.4	1.4	1.6%	1.9%	0.5%	0.5%	1.1%

Sources: USDA FAS GATS database; USDA Economic Research Service. Vegetable and Melon Yearbook 2011 and Fruit and Tree Nut Outlook 2012; U.S. National Fisheries Institute. "Top 10 Consumed Seafoods." 2012.

APPENDIX 2

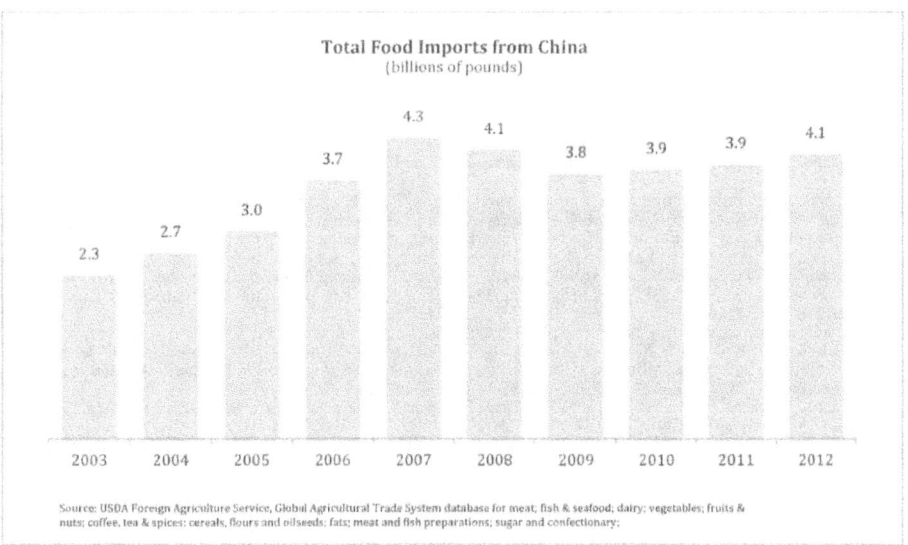

Total food imports from China fell during the economic recession, but over the past four years, imports have increased by about 250 million pounds, a 7 percent increase from 2009 to 2012.

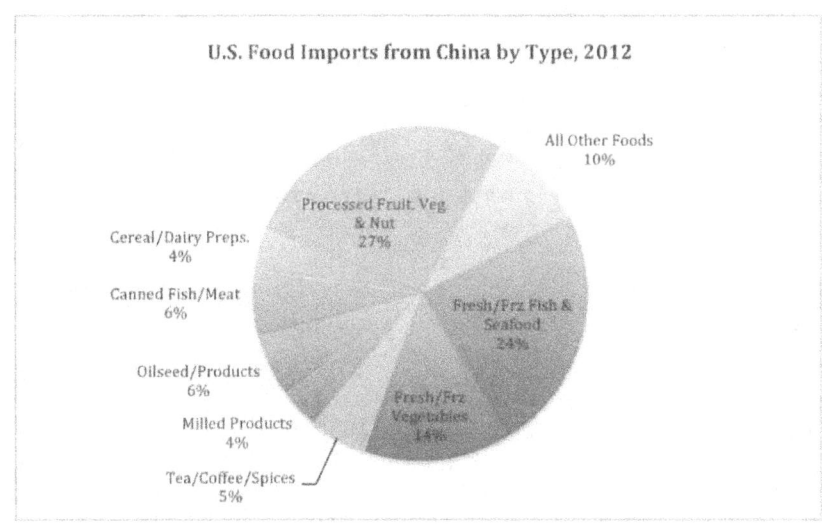

Source: USDA FAS GATS.

Fruits and vegetables (primarily frozen and processed) made up the plurality of imports from China, amounting to 1.6 billion pounds and 41 percent of the imported food products. The 1.2 billion in fresh, frozen and processed fish and seafood products made up about a third of the imports (30 perc

* * * * * * *

NOTES

[1] U.S. Government Accountability Office. ''Food Safety: FDA Can Better Oversee Food Imports by Assessing and Leveraging Other Countries' Oversight Resources.'' GAO–12–933. September 2012 at 1 and 5.

[2] U.S. Department of Agriculture Economic Research Service (USDA ERS). Table 1—Import Shares of US food consumption using the volume method. May 30, 2012. Available at http://www.ers.usda.gov/topics/international-markets-trade/us-agricultural-trade/import-share-of-consumption.aspx#import. Accessed April 22, 2013.

[3] Lohmar, Bryan et al. USDA ERS. ''China's Ongoing Agricultural Modernization.'' EIB–51. April 2009 at 1.

[4] United Nations Food and Agriculture Organization (UN FAO). FAOStat. Country rank in the world, by commodity (quantity): China. Based on most recent data available, 2008. Available at http://faostat.fao.org/. Accessed December 14, 2010.

[5] Barboza, David. "U.S. Court Fines Chinese Vitamin C Makers." *New York Times*. March 15, 2013.

[6] "Mix of chemicals may be key to pet-food deaths." CNN. May 1, 2007; U.S. Government Accountability Office. "Food and Drug Administration Overseas Offices have Taken Steps to Help Ensure Import Safety, but More Long-Term Planning is Needed." GAO–10–960. September 2010 at 1.

[7] Barboza, David and Alexei Barrionuevo. "Filler in Animal Feed is Open Secret in China." *New York Times*. April 30, 2007; Barboza, David. "Discovery of Melamine-Tainted Milk Shuts Shanghai Dairy." *New York Times*. January 2, 2010.

[8] "Mix of chemicals may be key to pet-food deaths." CNN. May 1, 2007.

[9] Barboza, David. "An Export Boom Suddenly Facing a Quality Crisis." *New York Times*. May 18, 2007; USDA. Press release. "Joint Update: FDA/USDA Update on Tainted Animal Feed." Release No. 0121.07. March 2, 2007.

[10] Gale, Fred and Jean Buzby. USDA ERS. "Imports from China and food safety issues." Economic Information Bulletin No. 52. July 2009 at 10.

[11] U.S. Department of Agriculture Foreign Agricultural Service (USDA FAS). Global Agricultural Trade System (HS–10: 2301000901, 2309100010.)

[12] Food and Drug Administration. Public Health Focus: Melamine Contamination in China. January 5, 2009. Available at http://www.fda.gov/NewsEvents/PublicHealthFocus/ucm179005.htm.

[13] Ee Lyn, Tan. "China eyes milk test after melamine deaths scandal." *Reuters*. June 15, 2010; Peterkin, Tom. "China milk scandal: 53,000 children fall ill from contaminated milk powder." *The (London) Telegraph*. September 22, 2008.

[14] Ee Lyn. June 15, 2010.

[15] Spears, Lee and Helen Yuan. "China withdraws milk as Fonterra decries Sanlu delay." *Bloomberg News*. September 24, 2008.

[16] Spencer, Richard. "China tainted milk scandal: Heinz and Mars drawn in." *The (London) Telegraph*. September 30, 2008; "Melamine found in Cadbury goods." *BBC*. September 29, 2008; "Melamine found in more Chinese-made food products." *New York Times*. September 26, 2008; Koo, Heejin. "South Korea orders Mars, Nestle to recall products." *Bloomberg News*. October 4, 2008; YUM! Brands. U.S. Securities and Exchange Commission. SEC filings 10–k. 2007 at 3. Spencer. *The (London) Telegraph*.

[17] US Honey Makers Take a Swat at Chinese Smugglers. Andrew Schneider. *AOL News*. May 6, 2010.

[18] Murphy, Joan. "Anti-dumping probe links large China shrimp exporter to transshipment." *Food Chemical News*. September 28, 2012.

[19] Food Sentry. Preliminary Analysis of International Food Safety Violations. Available at http://www.foodsentry.org/preliminary-analysis-of-international-food-safety-violations/. Accessed April 22, 2013.

[20] Baertlein, Lisa. "U.S. Shoppers Wary About China Food Safety: Survey" *Reuters*. January 19, 2011.

[21] "Nearly 70% of Chinese Consumers Do Not Trust Food Safety." *Arirang News*. January 3, 2011.

[22] USDA FAS. Global Agricultural Trade System. Available at www.fas.usda.gov/gats/. (Food includes consumption imports of meat; fish & seafood; dairy; vegetables, fruits & nuts, coffee, tea & spices; cereals, oil seeds; fats; meat & fish preparations; sugar & confectionery; cocoa; cereal & dairy preparations; vegetable & fruit preparations; and miscellaneous edible preparations contained in two-digit harmonized codes: HS–2: 02, 03, 04, 07, 08, 09, 10, 11, 12, 15, 16, 17, 18, 19, 20, 21, 22.)

[23] USDA FAS. Global Agricultural Trade System database for meat; fish & seafood; dairy; vegetables; fruits & nuts; coffee, tea & spices; cereals, flours and oilseeds; fats; meat and fish preparations; sugar and confectionery.

[24] USDA FAS. Global Agricultural Trade System.

[25] Gale, Fred et al. USDA Economic Research Service (ERS). "Investment in Processing Industry Turns Chinese Apples Into Juice Exports." FTS–344–01. October 2010 at 3.

[26] Gale and Buzby. USDA ERS. (2009) at iii; USDA FAS. Global Agricultural Trade System. USDA FAS GATS database; USDA ERS. Vegetable and Melon Yearbook 2011 and Fruit and Tree Nut Outlook 2012.

[27] USDA ERS. Fruit and Tree Nut Outlook Yearbook. 2010 at Table 16.

[28] USDA FAS. Global Agricultural Trade System. (Garlic, HS–10: 0703200020, 0703200010, 0712904040, 0712904020); USDA ERS. Vegetables and Melons Yearbook Data. 2009 (Updated May 20, 2010) at Table 5.

[29] Lee, Don. "China's additives on menu in U.S." *Los Angeles Times*. May 18, 2007.

[30] USDA FAS. Global Agricultural Trade System. (HS–10: 2912410000); Lee (2007).

[31] USDA FAS. Global Agricultural Trade System. (HS–6, 170490); Johnson, Tim. "China corners vitamin market." *Seattle Times*. June 3, 2007.

[32] USDA FAS. (HS–4, 1902 and 1905; HS–4, 2103; HS–10, 2309100090, 2039100010.)

[33] FDA. Import Refusal Database. Available at www.accessdata.fda.gov/scripts/importrefusals/. Accessed January–February 2011.

[34] FDA. Combined Field Activities—ORA. Program Activity Data. Field Foods Program Activity Data.

[35] Matsuda, Akane. "Food Safety Issues in the Vegetable Trade Between China and Japan: What Is Required to Establish Effective Food Safety Systems in the Bilateral Food Trade?" MPP Essay. Oregon State University, June 14, 2010.

[36] MacLeod, Calum. "China details new food-quality measures." *USA Today*. September 13, 2007.

[37] GAO (2010) at 12.

[38] Weisman, Steven. "China agrees to post U.S. safety officials in its food factories." *New York Times*. December 12, 2007; Zhe, Zhu. "U.S. food, drug agency opens Beijing office." *China Daily*. November 20, 2008.

[39] Lohmar, Bryan et al. USDA ERS. "China's Ongoing Agricultural Modernization." EIB–51. April 2009 at 24.

[40] Shames, Lisa. "Food Safety: FDA Could Strengthen Oversight of Imported Food by Improving Enforcement and Seeking Additional Authorities." GAO–10–699T. Testimony before the Subcommittee on Oversight and Investigations, U.S. House of Representatives Committee on Energy and Commerce. May 20, 2010 at 5.

[41] GAO. (2010) at 17.

[42] FDA. Combined Field Activities—ORA. Program Activity Data. Field Foods Program Activity Data.

[43] Food and Drug Administration. "CVM Issues Assignment to Collect and Analyze Samples of Pet Foods, Pet Treats, and Pet Nutritional Supplements in Interstate Commerce in the United States for *Salmonella*." March 22, 2013.

[44] Quaid, Libby. "U.S. to allow processed poultry shipments from China." *Associated Press*. April 20, 2006; 71 Fed. Reg. 20867–20871.

[45] Quaid. April 20, 2006; "U.S. tries to sell beef to China amid food disputes." *Reuters*. June 29, 2007.

[46] USDA Food Safety and Inspection Service. "Final report of an initial equivalence audit carried out in China covering China's poultry inspection system." May 17 2005 at 9–11.

[47] Pub. L. 110–161. Title VII. §733.

[48] World Trade Organization. "United States—Certain Measures Affecting Imports of Poultry from China: Report of the Panel." WT/DS392/R. September 29, 2010 at 183–184.

[49] "China to levy anti-dumping duty on U.S. Poultry." *Bloomberg News*. September 26, 2010.

[50] Oliphant, James. "Obama and Hu Jintao pledge cooperation, downplay differences." *Los Angeles Times*. January 19, 2011.

[51] Bottemiller, Helena. "USDA Petitioned to Block Chinese Poultry," *Food Safety News*. January 31, 2011.

[52] UPI. "China avian flu hits poultry sector, losses mount." April 16, 2013.

[53] Gale and Buzby (2009) at 17.

[54] Clapp, Stephen. "USDA bans organic certification agency from operating in China." *Food Chemical News*. June 21, 2010.

[55] U.S. Department of Agriculture National Organic Program (USDA NOP). "2010 Organic Assessment of China." July 2011 at 3.

[56] USDA NOP (2011) at 4.

[57] USDA NOP (2011) at 9.

[58] Clapp, Stephen. (2010).

[59] GAO (2012).

[60] GAO (2012) at 25.

[61] GAO (2012) at 19.

[62] "Food safety situation still grim in China." *Associated Press*. March 3, 2009.

[63] "Chinese lawmakers call for enhancing supervision of food safety." *Xinhua*. February 25, 2010.

[64] "China Releases Five Year Food Safety Plan." *Food Safety News*. June 18, 2012.

[65] Bodeen, Christopher. "Here we go again: China denies food safety Issues." *Associated Press*. May 23, 2007.

[66] Barboza and Barrionuevo (2007).

[67] "96 arrested in China for selling adulterated milk powder." IANS. January 13 2011.

[68] FDA. Import Refusal Report Database. Refusal Actions by FDA as Recorded in OASIS for China. January 2011. Accessed March 2, 2011 with code 72BCT99.

[69] Olesen, Alexa. "China warns dairy producers inspectors watching for toxic melamine and leather protein in milk." *Associated Press*. February 17, 2011.

[70] Olesen, Alexa. "Skinny pigs, poison pork: China battles farm drugs." *Associated Press*. January 24, 2011.

[71] USDA FAS. (HS–10: 04090000); FAO STAT. Country rank in the world, by commodity (quantity): China. Based on most recent data available, 2008. Accessed December 14, 2010.

[72] Schneider, Andrew. "Country of Origin no Guarantee on Cheap Imports." *Seattle Post-Intelligencer*. June 5, 2009.

[73] Fulton, April. "FDA seizes tainted Chinese honey after Sen. Schumer raises fuss." *National Public Radio*. June 11, 2010.

[74] Zhang, WenJun, FuBin Jiang, and Jiangfeng Ou. "Global pesticide consumption and pollution: with China as a focus." Proceedings of the International Academy of Ecology and Environmental Sciences. 2011. 1(2): 125–144.

[75] Wong, Edward. "Officials in China at odds over food scandal." *New York Times*. March 2, 2010.

[76] USDA FAS. International Maximum Residue Levels Database. Available at www.mrldatabase.com/. Accessed March 2011.

[77] "China vows harsh penalties for food safety crimes." *Associated Press*. September 16, 2010.

[78] "62,000 illegal food cases in 11 months of 2011." *Xinhua*. January 10, 2012.

[79] Ramzy, Austin. "China Food Safety: Big Crackdown, but Big Concerns Remain." *Time*. August 5, 2011.

[80] McDonald, Mark. "From Milk to Peas, A Chinese Food-Safety Mess." *International Herald Tribune*. June 21, 2012.

[81] Martina, Michael and Sally Huang. "Chinese police bust million-dollar rat-meat ring." *Reuters*. May 3, 2013.

[82] Barboza, David. "A Tide of Death, but This Time Food Supply Is Safe." *New York Times*. March 14, 2013.

[83] Yan, Wang. "Fake green peas latest food scandal." *China Daily*, China. March 31, 2010.

[84] "China media: Chinese liquor scandal." *BBC News*. November 22, 2012.

[85] Greenpeace. "Pesticides: Hidden Ingredients in Chinese Tea." 2012 at 1–2.

[86] Booth, Amy. "Residue concerns keep Chinese canned mushrooms off U.S. market." *Food Chemical News*. November 23, 2012.

[87] "Preserved fruit in China Tainted." *The New Paper*. April 30, 2012.

[88] "Chinese sellers accused of spraying cabbage with formaldehyde." *Associated Press*. May 7, 2012.

[89] Zuo, Mandy. "Dental cement used to calm fish." *South China Morning Post*. March 22, 2012.

[90] Gale and Buzby (2009) at 4.

[91] Wong. March 2, 2010.

[92] MacLeod, Calum. "China's organic farms rooted in food safety concerns." *USDA Today*. January 24, 2011.

[93] FDA. "FDA Investigates Animal Illnesses Linked to Jerky Pet Treats." September 14, 2012. http://www.fda.gov/AnimalVeterinary/SafetyHealth/ProductSafetyInformation/ucm319463.htm

[94] Aleccia, JoNel. "China stiff-arms FDA on jerky pet treat testing, reports show." NBCnews.com. August 22, 2012.

[95] FDA. Recall—Firm Press Release. "Milo's Kitchen Voluntarily Recalls Chicken Jerky and Chicken Grillers Homestyle Dog Treats." January 9, 2013.

[96] Crosse, Marcia. Testimony before the Senate Health, Education, Labor, and Pensions Committee. "Drug Safety: FDA Faces Challenges Overseeing the Drug Manufacturing Supply Chain." September 14, 2011. GAO–11–936T.

[97] U.S. Government Accountability Office. "Report to the Ranking Member, House Energy and Commerce Committee, Food and Drug Administration: Response to Heparin Contamination Helped Protect Public Health; Controls That Were Needed for Working with External Entities Were Recently Added." October 2010. GAO–11–95.

[98] U.S. Food and Drug Administration. "Information on Adverse Event Reports and Heparin." Available at http://www.fda.gov/Drugs/DrugSafety/PostmarketDrugSafetyInformationforPatientsandProviders/ucm112669.htm

---

PREPARED STATEMENT OF HON. SHERROD BROWN, A U.S. SENATOR FROM OHIO; CHAIRMAN, CONGRESSIONAL-EXECUTIVE COMMISSION ON CHINA

MAY 22, 2013

Thank you for attending this timely hearing. I'd like to thank the distinguished panelists for being here to help raise awareness about this important topic.

I'd also like to welcome the newest members of the Commission, Congressman Frank Wolf, Congressman Robert Pittenger, and Congressman Mark Meadows, and hope that the remaining appointments to the Commission will be made soon.

In recent months, the world has once again been reminded just how closely our health and safety is tied to China.

The current bird flu outbreak has claimed 36 lives and has spread to Taiwan.

The discovery of 20,000 dead pigs floating in Shanghai and rat meat being passed off as lamb have renewed concerns about the safety of China's food exports.

Pollution in Beijing and other cities has reached intolerable levels.

And this spring marks the height of the SARS crisis ten years ago, which took 774 lives and touched nearly every corner of the globe.

The risk to Americans has increased since we expanded trade relations with China without both providing for mechanisms to ensure safe imports, and without properly equipping our safety agencies with tools to ensure safe food.

In 2001, when China entered the World Trade Organization, the total amount of Chinese goods exported to the United States was $102 billion. In 2012, that number had reached a staggering $426 billion.

From 2001 to 2012, China's food exports to the United States reportedly tripled.

Between 2003 and 2011 the volume of pet food exports from China to the United States grew 85-fold.

Americans today might be surprised to learn just how much of their food and drugs are made in China. Some 80 percent of our tilapia, 50 percent of our apple juice, and 30 percent of our garlic comes from China.

This increased reliance on China has had grave consequences. In 2007, 149 Americans died after taking Heparin, a widely used blood thinner, linked to contaminants from Chinese workshops. Thousands of U.S. pets have died as a result of tainted treats from China.

Part of the problem is that some of our companies are all too willing to take advantage of China's lax safety standards, creating an un-level playing field for our home-grown producers.

But just as important has been China's failure to provide its citizens basic rights.

Chinese citizens lack the political freedom to elect officials responsive to their concerns.

There is no free press to help bring problems to public light

There are no independent courts to ensure officials and companies follow the law.

And there is no free civil society to sustain long-term advocacy.

The costs of the current Chinese system are clear both to the Chinese people and to consumers everywhere.

Without meaningful and effective pressure from their own citizens, Chinese officials still too often choose secrecy over openness and accountability.

Congress must also give close examination to our agencies responsible for safe drugs, food, and products and to the rules of international trade agreements, to ensure we do not lower standards.

I look forward to the testimony of our witnesses, and turn to Congressman Smith for his statement.

PREPARED STATEMENT OF HON. CHRISTOPHER SMITH, A U.S. REPRESENTATIVE FROM NEW JERSEY; COCHAIRMAN, CONGRESSIONAL-EXECUTIVE COMMISSION ON CHINA

MAY 22, 2013

Welcome to our distinguished witness to this hearing on the important issues of food and drug safety, public health, and the environment in China. I also want to thank the staff of this commission for their work to raise awareness about these three issues, as well as other human rights, rule of law, and governance issues.

Problems in the areas of food and drug safety, public health, and the environment deserve greater attention, research, and action; they affect countless people inside and outside of China. We hope to raise the visibility of these issues and that the Chinese government will respond in action, as well as words, to address the concerns of Chinese citizens and of all peoples who may be affected by imports of unsafe Chinese foods and drugs, by harmful pollution originating in China, or by public health crisis that take root in China.

While China has had impressive economic growth for decades, it lags behind in ensuring the rights of its citizens, and in developing transparency, official accountability, the rule of law, things it sourly needs to tackle these three issues.

Transparency is absolutely necessary for any government to protect the health of its citizens and to effectively manage problems related to food and drug safety, and public and environmental health. Therefore, it is unfortunate that it took about three weeks for Chinese health officials to make public information about the recent outbreak of bird flu.

It is also unfortunate that authorities continue to deny citizens information on the levels of soil contamination across the country, despite media and citizen requests for that information. Soil contamination has led to high levels of cadmium in at least 44 percent of the rice in at least one southern province. Authorities revealed the names of 8 brands which had been affected only after widespread criticism in the media and online regarding officials' original statement that it was ''not convenient to reveal'' the names of the brands. It is unconscionable for authorities to put the health of Chinese citizens at risk by withholding this information to protect the images of the government and specific companies.

In the past few months, over 20,000 pig carcasses have floated down rivers near Shanghai, but the Chinese government claims that there is no harm done to food or water quality. It is hard to get to the truth because central authorities are trying to control media coverage of these developments, telling journalists not to travel to locations to investigate. Keeping the media, citizens, and groups in the dark exacerbates food safety, health, and pollution problems.

The list of food and drug safety problems in China is long and continues to grow. Some of the glaring problems over the last few years include toxic preserved fruit, baby formula and milk tainted with melamine, and produce contaminated by pesticides, just to name a few. 94 million people in China become ill annually from food-borne diseases, and over 8,000 of these people die.

These safety problems affect Americans. Between 2006 and 2010, U.S. officials prevented some 9,000 unsafe Chinese products from entering the United States. Chinese authorities' attempts to reign in the problems have not worked. Major corruption scandals in the food and drug agencies over the last few years indicate the top-down accountability systems are not working.

The health of women due to the tragic forced abortions conducted under the coercive one-child policy which has been covered under previous hearings continues to cause tremendous pain and suffering both physical and emotional for millions.

Chinese leaders continue to make commitments to improve food and drug safety at some future date, but when people are getting sick and dying, patience is no longer possible.

Authorities in China need to be held accountable for implementing and enforcing laws the food and drug safety, public health, and environmental sectors. One of the ways to do that is to have authentic public oversight. Unfortunately, Chinese authorities continue to limit the growth of authentic civil society and citizen and group participation in policymaking and oversight processes is still very low.

Submission for the Record

Written Statement Submitted for the Record by Elizabeth Economy, C.V. Starr Senior Fellow and Director for Asia Studies, Council on Foreign Relations

May 22, 2013

China's Environmental Governance Crisis

Introduction

The Chinese government has traditionally placed limited value on transparency. Neither the political values of the Communist Party nor the institutional processes of the government inherently support sharing of information between the state and society or within the state itself. Recently, for example, the government announced that the results of a soil contamination survey indicated that 10 percent of all Chinese soil was contaminated with heavy metals and other pollutants. Yet it refused to release any further information on the grounds that the survey was a "state secret."[1] Transparency in China is unpredictable and episodic.

Nonetheless, within the past five years or so, the Chinese people have begun to demand greater transparency on issues that directly affect their well-being, such as the environment. Non-governmental organizations and the Internet increasingly bring the type of transparency that the people desire, sometimes working with, but more often working around, the country's formal political institutions.

To What Extent Is China Forthcoming?

The Chinese government does transmit some environmental information. The Ministry of Environmental Protection publishes an annual report with nationwide statistics on a range of issues, including water and air pollution, wastewater treatment, and land degradation. There is also a 2008 law designed to ensure that citizens have access to government information on environmental data. More recently, Beijing announced an initiative requiring that local governments above the county level inform the Ministry of Water Resources about construction projects in order to prevent salt water intrusion into strategic water reserves.[2]

Yet passing laws and announcing initiatives on transparency are not the same as actually implementing them. In 2005, the predecessor to the Ministry of Environmental protection, the State Environmental Protection Agency (SEPA), launched the Green GDP campaign, a project designed to calculate the costs of environmental degradation and pollution to local economies and provide a basis for evaluating the performance of local officials. Several provincial leaders balked, however, worried that the numbers would reveal the extent of the damage suffered by the environment under their leadership. SEPA's partner in the campaign, the National Bureau of Statistics (NBS), also undermined the effort by announcing that it did not possess the tools to do Green GDP accounting accurately, and that in any case it did not believe officials should be evaluated on such a basis. After releasing a partial report in September 2006, the NBS refused to release its subsequent findings. While the initiative appeared to lay dormant for a number of years, in 2013, following an air pollution crisis in Beijing and other Chinese cities, the *China Daily* published a piece calling for a renewed effort toward adopting a Green GDP, asserting, "It is generally believed that it is not technical limits but local governments that have prevented such data from being released. Such data releases might affect the promotion prospects of local officials. It is clear that if China wants to press on with the uphill task, it must first reshuffle its performance assessment methods for government officials."[3] The message is unequivocal: until local cadres are held accountable for the environment by the central government, the green implementation gap will remain.

---

[1] Christina Larson, "Soil Pollution Is a State Secret in China," Bloomberg BusinessWeek, February 25, 2013, www.businessweek.com/articles/2013–02–25/soil-pollution-is-a-state-secret-in-china.

[2] Elizabeth Economy, "The environment," in Handbook of China's Governance and Domestic Politics, ed. Chris Ogden, (New York, NY: Routledge, 2012), 199–209.

[3] China Daily, "Green GDP needed," February 27, 2013, http://www.chinadaily.com.cn/cndy/2013–02/27/content—16258973.htm.

A similar problem with implementation plagues other government initiatives. The two most established formal mechanisms—public participation in the review of environmental impact assessments (EIAs) and the citizen complaint system—are only spottily implemented. With regard to public participation in EIAs, as Chinese scholars have noted, there are a number of limitations: only a small percentage of projects are subjected to compulsory public participation; the timing and duration of engaging the public is short; the method of selecting those who can participate is often biased; and the amount of information actually disclosed is often quite limited in an effort to prevent social unrest.[4]

Chinese citizens also have the right to engage the system through a formal complaint system: writing letters to local environmental protection bureaus complaining of air, water, and waste pollution. According to the 2010 Environmental Statistical Yearbook, in 2010, there were over 700,000 such complaints.[5] During the 11th Five-Year Plan, the Ministry of Environmental Protection, itself, received 300,000 petitions on environmental matters. But resolution of these issues remains difficult. All told, there were only 980 administrative court cases about environmental impact assessments and only thirty criminal cases from 2006 to 2010. It is estimated that not even 1 percent of environmental disputes are resolved in court.[6]

HOW MUCH FREEDOM DO CHINESE PEOPLE HAVE TO MONITOR AND REPORT ON THESE ISSUES AND ADVOCATE FOR ENFORCEMENT?

If Beijing does not rigorously implement and enforce its environmental laws and regulations, Chinese non-governmental organizations (NGOs) and the Chinese people stand ready to intervene. Chinese environmental NGOs are at the forefront of pushing for greater transparency and disclosure. The Institute for Public Environment, headed by former journalist Ma Jun, for example, is renowned for its work in exposing multinationals whose supply chains often include small-scale factories that are violating environmental regulations. Once Ma uncovers a wrongdoing, he contacts the multinational and offers to work with it to get its environmental house in order. If the firm is unresponsive, he will use the Chinese media to shame the company into compliance. Greenpeace Beijing similarly applied the threat of media exposure to elicit change from large corporations, and successfully campaigned to persuade the supermarket group Metro to stop buying and selling Asia Pulp and Paper's rainforest-destroying paper products in China.

At the same time, some of the most challenging work in terms of bringing transparency to the environmental system is pursued on the legal front. Wang Canfa's Centre for Legal Assistance to Pollution Victims (CLAPV) is one of the very few resources for Chinese citizens who want to use a legal channel to pursue an environmental case. Over the past ten years, CLAPV has handled over 200 environmental lawsuits for pollution victims. In many instances, the media are an important ally in the NGO's fight for environmental protection, helping to shame polluters, uncover environmental abuse, and highlight environmental successes. Still, merely gaining access to the data to enable a case to be brought to trial remains a significant hurdle for many environmental lawsuits.

Beginning in 2009, Ma Jun also partnered with the U.S. NGO the Natural Resources Defense Council to launch an annual transparency index, which "ranks the performance of 113 major Chinese cities in complying with environmental disclosure requirements."[7] To accomplish this, they are using the 2008 law mandating transparency that Beijing, itself, could not effectively implement. While many cities still refuse to release the data—even though it is required by law—some Chinese officials have become fans of greater transparency as result of the NGO's work. One official from Hunan Province People's Congress uses his Weibo account to "name and shame" polluters, leading one named company to put in place new environmental clean-up technology.[8]

---

[4] Yuhuan Zhang, Xiaowen Liu, Yunjun Yu, Guojian Bian, Yu Li, and Yingxian Long, "Challenge of Public Participation in China's EIA Practice," (paper presented at the 32nd annual meeting of the International Association for Impact Assessment, Porto, Portugal, May 27–June 1, 2012).

[5] Ministry of Environmental Protection, "2010 Environmental Statistical Yearbook [2010 Nian Huanjing Tongji Nianbao]," http://wenku.baidu.com/view/b0111e88a0116c175f0e48d5.html.

[6] Feng Jie and Wang Tao, "Officials struggling to respond to China's year of environmental protests," China Dialogue, June 12, 2012, http://www.chinadialogue.net/article/show/single/en/5438-Officials-struggling-to-respond-to-China-s-year-of-environment-protests-

[7] Barabara Finamore, Wang Yan, Wu Qi, and Christine Xu, "A Step Forward for Environmental Transparency in China," National Resources Defense Council Staff Switchboard Blog, March 29, 2013, www.switchboard.nrdc.org/blogs/bfinamore/a—step—forward—for—environment.html.

[8] Ibid.

The advent of the Internet has further contributed to the ability of the Chinese people to apply bottom-up pressure for change, and has provided an unprecedented level of transparency in the environmental system, resulting in Internet petitions, water pollution maps demarcating polluting factories, and pictures of polluted sites or protesting Chinese. Urban residents also have become skilled at using the Internet and mobile phone text messaging to organize environmental protests.

In one celebrated case, the Internet became a lightning rod for coalescing public opinion against local government regulations and resulted in a change in policy. On December 5–6, 2011, smog forced the cancellation of almost 700 flights at Beijing Capital Airport and ignited a media firestorm. The Beijing Municipal Bureau of Environmental Protection had reported the air pollution on December 5 as "light."[9] However, the U.S. Embassy in Beijing, which had been Tweeting air quality numbers for several months, recorded the pollution level as 'beyond index.' There were important differences in the pollutants on which Beijing reported (PM_{10}) and those on which the U.S. Embassy reported ($PM_{2.5}$ and ozone), and how each rated air quality, with the United States supporting tougher standards and metrics. Under pressure from China's online citizens, or netizens, the local Beijing environmental officials agreed to revamp their system by 2016 to report on additional pollutants. Yet that did not satisfy local residents. Real estate billionaire Pan Shiyi conducted an online poll and discovered that 91 percent of the more than 40,000 respondents believed that the government should immediately match the U.S. Embassy's reporting quality. One month later Beijing started to report on its air quality with the same statistical measures as the U.S. Embassy (albeit only from one site in the city). Moreover, on March 1, 2012, Beijing announced that it would extend its air pollution monitoring network to all major cities including Shanghai, Chongqing, and Tianjin in 2012, as well as incorporating 113 additional cities in 2013.[10] By 2015, China plans to have all medium-to-large cities monitoring and reporting on their $PM_{2.5}$ levels. Even China's official news agency, *Xinhua*, commented that social networking sites such as Weibo played an important role in spurring central leaders to take action on the issue.[11]

Occasionally, even the government has begun to take advantage of the Internet to garner support for particular initiatives. For example, in the highly contentious South-North Water Transfer Project, netizens on the nationalistic and popular "Strengthening the Nation" online forum generally support the project, with some even arguing that cutting of the Yarlung Tsangpo river would not only help solve China's water shortage problems but also "force India to compromise over disputed territory by controlling their water flow."[12] At the same time, the Ministry of Water Resources, which does not support the third leg of the project, used the Internet to publish a series of articles less supportive of the project. Discussion on the project on their website was largely negative, with some referring to Western sources such as Jared Diamond and a movie about the National Parks Service to support their cause for why the project should not move forward.

The Internet also serves as an organizational tool for Chinese citizens to spread information regarding protests. The lack of an effective institutional mechanism for the Chinese people to participate in the environmental policy-making process or to get redress through the legal system has translated into a vibrant environmental protest movement in China. When citizens' concerns are not addressed satisfactorily, they turn to protest to make their voices heard, either via the Internet or on the street. The environment has now surpassed illegal land expropriation as the leading source of social unrest in the China.[13]

In some cases, protests are virtual via the Internet. In late 2010, Chinese netizens broke the story of a significant environmental disaster in Jilin province, where thousands of barrels of pollutants had been dumped into a water source by a local chemical plant. In the ten days that it took Chinese officials to admit to the disaster, thousands of citizens were informed of the cover-up via the Internet. They re-

[9] Lousia Lim, "Clean Air A 'Luxury' In Beijing's Pollution Zone," NPR.org, December 7, 2011, http://www.npr.org/2011/12/07/143214875/clean-air-a-luxury-in-beijings-pollution-zone.

[10] Xinhua, "PM2.5 in air quality standards, positive response to net campaign," March 1, 2013, http://news.xinhuanet.com/english/china/2012–03/01/c—122773759.htm.

[11] Elizabeth Economy, "The environment," in Handbook of China's Governance and Domestic Politics, ed. Chris Ogden.

[12] Strengthening the Nation Blog, "Make the Brahmaputra River Flow into the Yangtze, the Distance Will Be the Smallest and the Benefits Will Be the Largest [Yin Yalucangbujiang Zhi Shuiru Changjiang Zhi Yuan, Juli Zuidian Xiaoyi Zuigao]", February 8, 2009, http://bbs1.people.com.cn/postDetail.do?view=2&pageNo=1&treeView=0&id=90600434&boardId=2.

[13] Bloomberg News, "Chinese Anger Over Pollution Becomes Main Cause of Social Unrest," March 6, 2013, http://www.bloomberg.com/news/2013–03–06/pollution-passes-land-grievances-as-main-spark-of-china-protests.html.

sponded by purchasing a massive amount of bottled water and angrily denouncing the government's inaction. It was only after the citizens refused to believe the official stories that the government finally acknowledged the disaster and handed out free bottles of water to those in the afflicted areas.[14] Similarly, a year earlier in Guangzhou, online transparency caused a reversal in local government policy. Middle class-led protests over a planned incinerator were picked up by young online netizens, who then spread the news through social media websites. Even though the activists themselves were not affected by the plans, they wanted the word to get out. Once enough citizens became involved, the government agreed to halt the project until a full environmental assessment was completed.[15]

Even more threatening to authorities is the potential for environmental protest to spread from one city to another. In July 2012, for example, protests broke out in the southwestern province of Sichuan, where citizens of the small city of Shifang were upset by a planned molybdenum copper plant. The facility would be a $1.64 billion project funded by the Sichuan Hongda Company,[16] but residents of Shifang, led by students and joined by others from nearby towns and cities, feared that the plant would have a negative impact on the environment and their health.[17] The state-supported *Global Times* estimated that several thousand protestors took part in the protests,[18] which turned violent, forcing the police to use tear gas and stun grenades to disperse the crowds.[19] Thirteen protestors were injured [20] and another twenty-seven were detained during the protests, of which six were formally charged.[21] On the third day of demonstrations, local officials announced that the project would be halted.[22]

Later that month, inspired by Internet reports of the Shifang protest, thousands of protesters took to the streets in Qidong, a coastal city in the province of Jiangsu, to challenge a pipeline that would discharge waste into the sea and potentially pollute a nearby fishery, as well as contaminate drinking water.[23] Worried that wastewater originating from the Japan's Oji Paper Company in Nantong city would not be cleaned properly, a thousand or more protestors (*Reuters* reported there were about 1,000,[24] while the *Asahi Shimbum* estimated 10,000[25]) damaged government buildings, cars, and property on July 27.[26] Some demonstrators clashed with police, and at least one police car was overturned; hundreds of police arrived later in the day to protect government offices.[27] Fourteen people plead guilty to encouraging the riot in which dozens of police were injured; the local Communist party chief was stripped half-naked; and protestors caused more than $20,000 of damage.[28]

Public transparency may have reached a new high in May 2013, when Kuming, the capital city of the southwestern province of Yunnan, was rocked by protests over plans by China National Petroleum Corporation (CNPC) and the Yuntianhua Group to build a refinery in a nearby city of Anning. Kunming's mayor Li Wenrong took the unusual step of announcing that the government would cancel the project if

[14] Elizabeth Economy and Jared Mondschein, ''China: the New Virtual Political System,'' CFR.org (April 2011), http://www.cfr.org/china/china-new-virtual-political-system/p24805.

[15] Malcolm Moore, ''China's middle-class rise up in environmental protest,'' The Telegraph, November 23, 2009, http://www.telegraph.co.uk/news/worldnews/asia/china/6636631/Chinas-middle-class-rise-up-in-environmental-protest.html.

[16] Brian Spegele, ''Planned China Metals Plant Scrapped,'' Wall Street Journal, July 3, 2012, http://online.wsj.com/article/SB10001424052702304211804577504101311079594.html.

[17] BBC, ''China factory construction halted amid violent protests,'' July 3, 2012, http://www.bbc.co.uk/news/world-asia-china-18684895.

[18] Ibid.

[19] Spegele, ''Planned China Metals Plant Scrapped.''

[20] BBC, ''China factory construction halted amid violent protests.''

[21] Caixin Online, ''Timeline of Shifang Protests,'' July 5, 2012, http://english.caixin.com/2012–07–05/100407585.html.

[22] Ibid.

[23] Jane Perlez, ''Waste Project Is Abandoned Following Protests in China,'' The New York Times, July 28, 2012, http://www.nytimes.com/2012/07/29/world/asia/after-protests-in-qidong-china-plans-for-water-discharge-plant-are-abandoned.html?—r=0.

[24] John Ruwitch, ''China cancels waste project after protests turn violent,'' Reuters, July 28, 2012, http://www.reuters.com/article/2012/07/28/us-china-environment-protest-idUSBRE86R02Y20120728.

[25] Bloomberg News, ''Chinese City Halts Waste Project After Thousands Protest,'' July 29, 2012, http://www.bloomberg.com/news/2012–07–29/chinese-city-halts-plant-s-waste-project-after-thousands-protest.html.

[26] Ibid.

[27] Ibid.

[28] Associated Press, ''Chinese protesters plead guilty after water pollution riot in Qidong,'' January 21, 2013, http://www.guardian.co.uk/world/2013/jan/31/china-wastewater-pollution-riots-qidong.

"most of our citizens say no to it."[29] In essence, Li was inviting a public referendum on the project.

In virtually every instance of environmental protest in urban areas, local governments respond by acceding to the demands of the protestors. According to Ma Jun, director of the Institute of Public Environment in Beijing, "The next leadership of China is going to face a challenge on these environmental issues, which the previous leadership had not seen so strongly for thirty years. For the first time, some local officials have begun to call us to learn more about how these situations are handled in other countries—they really worry about becoming the next protest targets."[30]

CONCLUSION

The Chinese government appears at a loss as to how to manage the growing push from below for greater environmental transparency. Ignoring the people's demands comes with a high price: growing societal discontent and rising numbers of mass protests. Thus far, the leadership appears willing to pay the cost. However, the long-term effects—both on the environment and the leaders' own legitimacy—will only continue to grow.

* The Council on Foreign Relations takes no institutional positions on policy issues and has no affiliation with the U.S. government. All statements of fact and expressions of opinion contained herein are the sole responsibility of the author.

---

[29] Xinhua, "Public opinion decisive in Kunming's controversial chemical project: mayor," May 10, 2013, www.globaltimes.cn/content/780724.shtml#.UZOCorXU-84.
[30] Christina Larson, "Protests in China Get a Boost From Social Media," Bloomberg BusinessWeek, October 29, 2012, http://www.businessweek.com/articles/2012-10-29/protests-in-china-get-a-boost-from-social-media.